SURREY
MURDER
CASEBOOK

W. H. JOHNSON

COUNTRYSIDE BOOKS
NEWBURY · BERKSHIRE

COUNTRYSIDE BOOKS
3 Catherine Road
Newbury, Berkshire

To view our complete range of books,
please visit us at
www.countrysidebooks.co.uk

ISBN 1 85306 642 7

Designed by Graham Whiteman

Produced through MRM Associates Ltd., Reading
Typeset by Techniset Typesetters, Newton-le-Willows
Printed by J. W. Arrowsmith Limited, Bristol

CONTENTS

ACKNOWLEDGEMENTS

I have to thank many people for their practical assistance and advice in the writing of this book. Criminologists and true-crime writers offered generous assistance from their own researches; police officers considered drafts and saved me from making some serious errors; librarians were unfailingly patient when I wrote to them or telephoned with requests for help; and newspaper readers responded generously to my appeals for information. I have rarely met with such willingness to help a complete stranger.

My thanks and gratitude, then, are due to the following in no particular order of merit: friends in the Police History Society, especially Alan Hayhurst and Dr Jenny Ward; Mrs Gerry Middleton-Stewart, Head of Registry, Surrey Police HQ; Syd Groombridge; Brian Lane; serving and retired Surrey police officers, particularly ex-Superintendent Fred Shoobridge who investigated the Chalk Pit murder over 50 years ago; Paul Williams whose cuttings service, *Murder Files*, saved me so much foot-slogging; the staff of the Surrey History Centre, Woking; David Orchard; Roger Packham; and as ever the amiably patient staff of Eastbourne Central library.

Let me single out two people who have been especially helpful to me. They are John Collard of South Godstone and former Chief Superintendent Bob Bartlett. They have been absolute gems. Like all of the others mentioned, they are of course absolved from any flaws and inaccuracies in these accounts.

The work on two of the cases described here was made easier by two meticulously researched, elegantly written books. I refer to Richard Whittington-Egan's *Riddle of Birdhurst Rise* and *The Wigwam Murder* by MJ Trow. Both books are models of their kind and I am grateful to both authors.

For any whose copyright I have failed to trace may I apologise in advance. Any omissions will be amended in future printings.

INTRODUCTION

The murders described in this book did not all occur within the present boundaries of Surrey. The first case, the gruesome account of Kate Webster's murder of her mistress, took place in Richmond but at the time, 1879, that town was part of the county. And in 1928 and 1929, when three members of one family were poisoned, Croydon also belonged to Surrey. I hope that this will satisfy those purists who insist that I ought to have stuck to today's county limits. But had I so restricted myself I should have robbed the reader of two absorbing tales.

Then there is the more recent case of John Shippey. In 1991 he was murdered in Croydon which has for many years been a London Borough, but my justification for including this particular account is that the body was discovered near Merstham which led to the investigation being conducted by the Surrey police force.

So much for explanation.

This collection of cases includes some which might be called classics, murders which across the years have been much discussed and written about. The Merstham Tunnel Murder, the Wigwam Murder, the Warlingham Chalk Pit case and of course Kate Webster's murky deed all fall into this category. But I have also sought out other less well known cases. Several are much more recent and whilst they claimed their share of the newspapers they have not for the most part previously appeared in book form.

I have wondered greatly about the degrees of wickedness of those who come within these covers. During my researches I have in a sense lived with them and have tried to understand what drove them to their crimes. I have no doubt that several of those whose deeds are presented here were mad rather than bad. I think, too, that there was in one instance an unintentional killing which nevertheless led two men to the scaffold. Elsewhere greed plays a disproportionately great part in the lives and deaths of some of them. And lust, too. But I really believe that there are some deeply wicked men and women here. There is at least one, possibly two, who will rank with the great monsters whose names have stayed with us down the years: I have George Joseph

Smith and Neville Heath in mind and the likes of Neill Cream, Haigh, Christie and of course the immortal, most awful Jack.

I close still tussling with questions that have stayed with me for so long. What is it that intrigues us about such dreadful crimes? Why do murderers going about their work weave such compelling spells? Sometimes I tell myself that it is because murder is rarely dull, that it has a powerful narrative drive, that it is like the best fiction. But also I must admit other questions. Is it that in these fearsome acts we sometimes see some faint reflections of our own darkest thoughts, our most disturbing nightmares? Is that the secret of murder's compulsion?

W. H. Johnson

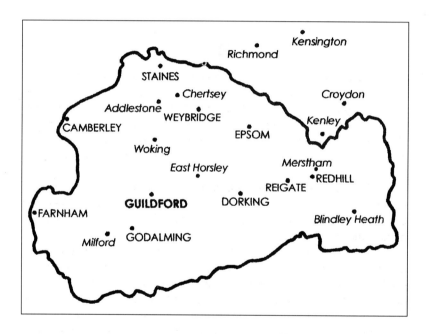

1

A
SERVANT PROBLEM

The Murder of Julia Martha Thomas at Richmond,
March 1879

Now, let's just get this straight. The woman did *not* go round the Richmond pubs selling jars of dripping made from human flesh. That's just saloon bar talk. It's macabre. Mrs Hayhoe, landlady at The Hole in the Wall in Park Road, apparently spread that tale but it's just not true. Yes, there *was* something in the black leather bag. She threw that away but what it was, there is no knowing. And, yes, it has to be admitted that they never found the head.

And another thing to get straight is what to call her. We'll use the name they used in court. To us, she's Kate Webster. Neither Webb nor Gibbs; neither Shannon nor Lawless. Not Lawler which was her real name. And not Thomas.

So here comes Kate, on 4th March 1879, up to the door of the Porter family in Hammersmith. And she's a very grand lady now, silk dress, gold watch on a chain, rings, jewellery. Anne Porter didn't recognise her at first, didn't know her till she spoke in that strong County Wexford accent. She had never seen her so splendidly arrayed before. She was never like that when she worked next door. She was just a skivvy then. Anne hadn't seen her for such a time. How her fortunes had changed.

Well, Kate tells Anne that she's just come over from Richmond by train because she wants a word with Mr Porter. He's at work at the moment, Anne says, but she invites her in for a chat about old times. She tells her how Porter's doing well at the painting and decorating and the boy, young Bob, is with his father at the trade now. And Anne recalls Kate's kindness in those times past when she took such a loving interest in the Porter's little girl, now, alas, no longer with us. The chat goes on and they break a bottle that Kate has brought and they send out for a half of gin because Kate enjoys a glass, no doubt about that, and so does Anne Porter who, truth to tell, enjoys just a little too much. Then Porter comes in and the boy with him. And Kate tells them all about the changes in her fortunes.

Kate says she's widowed now. She's Mrs Thomas, living in Park Road in Richmond. At 2 Vine Cottages, semi-detached and very respectable. Anyway, an aunt has passed on leaving her very comfortably off what with the furniture and the house. She's decided against staying and all she wants now is to go back to Ireland. Her father's ill and wants her back. So does Mr Porter in his line of business know of anyone who'll buy her furniture or who'll sell it for her? She doesn't know anybody in Richmond, she says, and you have to careful in these sorts of matters. And Porter thinks he might just have the right feller in mind. He'll let her know.

Well, time flies and Kate has to be off. The Porter men, William and young Bob, say they'll walk part of the way back with her. And anyway, she's got that ever so heavy black leather bag. Good God, they probably say in a joking sort of way, what ever have you got in there? You got the crown jewels or something? You'd think it had weights in it. And they insist on carrying it because it's too much for a woman, even a big, strong, raw-boned young woman like Kate. So between them the two men carry the black bag.

They walk as far as the Hammersmith suspension bridge and call in to The Oxford and Cambridge pub. Then Kate says she has to meet a friend in Barnes, just over the other side of the bridge. She won't be long, she says, and off she goes with the bag. Twenty minutes later she's back minus the bag. But now she's sporting five fine rings which the friend has given her. Actually, Kate tells them, they belonged to her sister who'd died and this friend has been keeping them for her.

But now it's getting dark and Kate asks if his father will allow young Bob to accompany her to Vine Cottages. And Porter agrees. They can take the new District Line and Bob can be home in no time after he's done escort duty. Up at Vine Cottages, perhaps at about ten o'clock, Kate is in no hurry to dismiss the boy and probably at 15 years of age and after working with his father all day, he's in no hurry to go. Kate's pleased with life. Look at these, she says, showing him her pass books from the Monarch Building Society and the Post Office Savings Bank. In her name, of course. Mrs Thomas.

There is one other thing, Kate says to the lad. She'd be ever so grateful if he could give her a hand. She knows it's late but she has another box to take to a friend of hers. She'd really like to take it tonight. Would he mind? And of course he's willing to help her because she's an old friend of the family.

But it's a struggle all the way to the bridge at Richmond. It's about three quarters of a mile along Park Road and then Mount Ararat Road before they cut down to the river. This white deal box, tied with rope, is quite small but it's heavy even for the two of them. And it's made extra difficult because it has only one handle. But at last they're on the bridge and when they reach one of the recesses on the left hand side, on the Twickenham side of the river, Kate tells Bob to leave. 'You run back,' she says. 'I'll soon catch you.'

And the boy runs back. He's swallowed Kate's tale that she's meeting her friend because he probably thinks that's the way adults behave at eleven o'clock at night. Or perhaps he tells himself, maybe that's how the Irish act. And as he runs back he hears a splash in the water. A barge, he tells himself.

In a minute or two Kate's back with him. He's missed the last train, she tells him, but he can sleep at Vine Cottages tonight which is what he does do. And it's all very chaste and he gets home safe early next morning.

That same morning, at about seven o'clock, Henry Wheatley, a coal porter, sees a small box bobbing on the water near Barnes bridge, five miles or so from Richmond. He thinks his luck is in. He's not one to pass up what might be something valuable. So he fishes out the box. Inside are some parcels, each wrapped in strong brown paper. And inside there is what at first sight looks like meat. He wonders if it isn't some student prank but he calls the police just in case. At the mortuary the incomplete remains of a woman are examined.

There is nothing to indicate who is lying on the slab. No one locally has been reported missing. What can be said is that one piece of flesh has been boiled. It's all been tightly packed in that little deal box. There is part of the chest, the heart, a piece of lung and some parts of a leg, an arm and a left foot. There is no head.

And now back to Kate. Perhaps here might be a good place to fill in some background. She was, in 1879, 30 years of age with a history of criminal offences. She'd done time in Ireland for larceny as well as in England where she had served several prison terms, one in Newgate. She had done one four-year stretch and in 1875 had received 18 months at Surrey Assizes for 36 offences of theft. She had been most recently released after another twelve months imposed in February 1877. Kate specialised in lodging house thefts, taking a room and then after a few days, disappearing with whatever took her fancy. Gaol-hardened by the time she showed up at Vine Cottages in January 1879, her sole aim was to carry out her usual con trick. Though she had an undoubtedly glib tongue, she was regularly found out in a short time. She really was not a good enough thief or liar though she was well enough practised.

Quite by chance Kate had been offered the job at Vine Cottages by Mrs Julia Martha Thomas, a tartar of a woman, who could never keep her servants. She was so demanding that whoever she employed upped and awayed as soon as they possibly could. And in January 1879 Mrs Thomas's cook-general had left her in the lurch. Desperate, she told a friend of her problem and the friend who had employed the young Irish woman for a day or so in an emergency passed on the name of Kate Webster. So on 27th January, after a cursory interview, Kate took up her appointment in the small semi that Mrs Thomas rented from Miss Ives, living next door at 1 Vine Cottages.

It was an ideal sort of place, Kate must have thought. The old lady – she was in her mid-fifties – had elegant dresses and some fine jewellery. The furniture, too, was decent enough though the bulk of it belonged not to Mrs Thomas but to her landlord.

Things appear not to have worked out from the start. Not that that would have worried Kate who was indifferent to her mistress's opinions. But she was exasperated by Mrs Thomas playing the piano, quite the lady, while she scrubbed floors, polished brasses, swilled the front step, cooked the meals. And there were two paying guests there for a couple of weeks. More work.

Mrs Thomas was apparently soon dissatisfied enough with her latest acquisition. Her diary for 28th February reads: 'Gave Katherine warning to leave.' If Kate was to make much out of this place, she would have to get a move on. But she was planning her departure prior to receiving notice. On 25th February Kate had visited a friend, Mary Durden, a straw bonnet maker who lived in Kingston. Kate said her circumstances were due to change very soon. She was going to inherit property from an aunt in Birmingham. There was jewellery, too, and a gold watch and chain. And furniture to sell. She'd be off shortly to settle matters. Her aunt was dying. By the time she got there Kate expected she'd be dead.

Three days later she was back in Kingston, this time to Acre Street, where the father of Johnny, her five year old son, lived. Could he get her some sugar of lead? He could and did from a local chemist. But the poison was never used.

On 28th February, Mrs Thomas's paying guests, Mrs Menhennick and her daughter, from Raynes Park, left. The house was quieter. But from Sunday, 2nd March, Kate was busier than ever. She had gone out on the Sunday afternoon and had too much to drink. When she came back she and Mrs Thomas had a row. From her demeanour that evening at the Presbyterian chapel, Mrs Thomas was evidently upset. Kate's confession describes what happened next.

'Upon her return from church, before her usual hour, she came in and went upstairs. I went up after her, and we had an argument which ripened into a quarrel, and in the height of my anger and rage, I threw her from the top of the stairs to the ground floor. She had a heavy fall. I felt that she was seriously injured, and I became agitated at what had occurred, lost all control of myself and to prevent her from screaming or getting me into trouble, I caught her by the throat and in the struggle she was choked.'

The general view, however, is that Mrs Thomas was struck on the back of the head with a meat cleaver. After the trial at an auction of household effects, a cleaver, claimed by the auctioneer to be the suspected weapon, went for five shillings.

The confession continues: 'I determined to do away with the body as best I could. I chopped the head from the body with the assistance of a razor which I used to cut through the flesh afterwards. I also used the meat saw and the carving knife to cut the body up with. I prepared the copper with water to boil the body to prevent identity, and as soon as I succeeded in cutting it up I placed it in the copper and boiled it. I opened the stomach with the carving knife and burned up as much of the parts as I could.'

And so all through the night and into the next dawn Kate cuts, hacks, saws and slices. She struggles through bone, muscle, gristle and ligament. The copper is on and she boils flesh and clothing. Onto the kitchen fire she throws flesh and gut, sinew and bone. She scrubs floor boards, tables, knives, cupboards. Her hands, wrists and arms are crimsoned; her apron, her cheeks, her boots are spattered with reds and pinks, yellows and creams as she labours in the stench of it.

'I was greatly overcome, both from the horrible sight before me and the smell, and I failed several times in my strength and determination, but was helped on by the Devil.'

11

Early on the Monday, 3rd March, Miss Jane Ives at 1 Vine Cottages, saw a light next door. At seven o'clock she heard the sound of washing and brushing in next door's scullery and the copper being poked and riddled. Not that that was the only sound she'd heard. The night before there had been what she had taken for a chair being knocked over in the hall. By eleven o'clock in the morning the washing was out on the back garden line. So much early industry. And Miss Ives also remarked upon the smell!

There were other matters that Kate had to deal with on that Monday. The coal man called with his bill. Mrs Thomas wasn't at home, Kate told him. Then Mrs Roberts, one of Mrs Thomas' friends, called round but Kate didn't answer the door. Miss Ives sent round her servant girl on the Tuesday to tell Mrs Thomas that the men were coming to repair a leak. No need, Kate told her. It had been the melting snow, but there was nothing to repair.

It was that same Tuesday, 4th March, that Kate visited her old friends the Porters. And she made a new friendship with Jack Church, a friend of the Porters and owner of The Rising Sun beershop, just a few doors away from where the Porters lived. Over the next week he and Porter went to Vine Cottages several times to estimate the value of the furniture. It is hard to believe that Kate was other than a poor but compulsive liar for she told Church that she was going to Scotland to

Vine Cottages where the murder took place.

live with her father, a Glasgow solicitor. She told a similar story to another friend. How she kept the stories going with the Porters, who thought she was off to live with her sick father in Ireland, is difficult to understand.

Church, who had some business acumen – at least he had up to £500 in his bank account – was to allege that he thought Kate had a good business head on her shoulders. He took on the arrangements to have the furniture removed and sold elsewhere. He intended to buy some of the items himself and send off the rest to auction. Over several days he removed some of the furniture – tablecloths, mats, glass from chandeliers, vases, carving knives and forks, candlesticks, plates and curtains – to The Rising Sun.

From 10th March, Church, a married man, called on Kate every day, taking her out for drinks, she in her satin-trimmed beefeater hat and the large earrings that Church bought her. The couple spent hours alone together in the house although she slept at nights at the Porters, where little Johnny was now installed.

And nobody yet suspected that the remains washed up at Barnes bridge had anything to do with Mrs Thomas. And nobody suggested that the ankle and foot found on an allotment dunghill at Copthall in Twickenham on 10th March had anything to do with the former occupier of 2 Vine Cottages. Yes, busy though she was, Kate still had had time to make her way to Twickenham.

But if no one suspected that Julia Thomas had been done away with, the neighbours had become increasingly curious. They had not seen her for days. And the servant and her behaviour were causing concern. She was in and out of the house every day with parcels, and at nights she was never home. One day they saw her arm-in-arm with a man going into the house. Other times during the day they had seen a man with a notebook going round the house and on at least one occasion they had heard the piano and singing. What on earth could Julia Thomas be thinking of?

If the neighbours were concerned they were not suspicious of anything like murder. Miss Ives had heard things, of course, but murder never entered her head. And Porter, who sold a set of false teeth for Kate – he got £6 for them – never suspected Kate of such a crime. And friends who wrote and had no reply and others who called at the house, equally unsuccessfully, were no more than slightly puzzled.

And through it all, Kate Webster arranges the selling of her furniture, arranges for Johnny to stay at the Porters where she joins him at nights, meets Church for drinks and the pursuit of a short-lived love affair. Does she not think of the other awful matter? Doesn't she dream?

On Monday, 17th March, with Church's help, Kate spent much of the day packing, getting things ready for the furniture removal the following day. And the next day Weston's two horse-drawn vans turned up at 2 Vine Cottages. Then in the middle of the task out came Miss Ives calling out that they had no right to be taking the furniture from the house. It was hers, she said. 'And where is Mrs Thomas?' she demanded. If Porter and Church did not then realise that Kate had assumed her former mistress's identity, they certainly smelt a rat.

'You have deceived me,' Church told Kate. 'I will have nothing to do with the goods. Put them back again.'

And while the furniture was being carried back inside, Kate disappeared, finding a hansom round the corner to take her to The Rising Sun. Doubtless Mrs Church was surprised to see her. Wasn't she moving today? Wasn't her husband with Mr Porter at Vine Cottages? Kate spun a tale for she was quick-witted in such circumstances. And could Mrs Church let her borrow a sovereign for some or other emergency? And Mrs Church, poor trusting soul, came up with the cash.

Off then to the Porters' house where doubtless Mrs Porter was equally amazed to see Kate. But no, Kate wanted Johnny with her. He had been with the Porters for the last ten days and now it appeared she'd like to take him to Richmond.

And then she was off again. But where? When they returned from

THE MURDERED LADY Mrs THOMAS (From A Photo)

THE PRISONER. KATE WEBSTER.

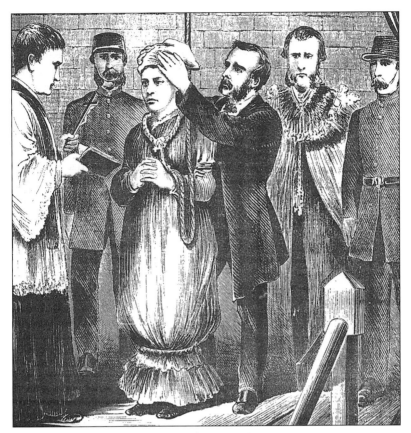

The execution of Kate Webster.

Richmond, Porter and Church compared tales with their wives and could not satisfactorily explain what on earth was going on.

Days later, however, a dress and a hat box which had been delivered by the removal men to Church's house helped solve the mystery.

On 21st March, Mrs Church, inspecting the dress, found a letter in the pocket from Mrs Julia Thomas' friend, Mrs Menhennick of Raynes Park. Perhaps, Church and Porter agreed, she might be able to resolve the mystery. Off they went to Raynes Park. What they heard there was that their Mrs Thomas, a 30 year old, with her liking for gin and her little boy, was nothing like Mrs Menhennick's old friend. This was a police matter.

When the police searched the house they found hand bones hidden

15

under the copper furnace and under the kitchen grate. In the copper there was some fatty matter. There were smears of blood on the staircase, in the pantry and in the back bedroom. Evidently an attempt to boil and burn the body had been abandoned. There was a chopper and a razor.

A week or so later a lady who had announced herself as the widow of Captain J. W. Webster and the mother of four children, was arrested at Killaun in County Wexford by detectives from London. She was returned to Richmond and charged with murder.

In the course of a six-day trial Kate Webster tried unsuccessfully to pin responsibility on Jack Church, on Porter and on the father of her child. Whilst it was a complex case, with 53 witnesses, confused with all the more or less innocent arrangements with the marvellously imprudent Church and the astonishing naivete of the Porter family, Kate was condemned to death.

On 29th July 1879, Kate Webster was hanged at Wandsworth. She had really gained little from her crime, which was not the rash act of temper which she claimed. She intended that Julia Thomas would die. But all she got out of it was £6 for a set of teeth; £11 10s which she found in the house; Church's £18 deposit on the furniture and only the promise of a balance of £60. And of course, a few drinks on the way.

2

THE
DESPERATE FAILURE

The Murder of Isaac Frederick Gold between
Merstham Tunnel and Earlswood,
June 1881

At 3.30 pm on Monday 27th June 1881, when the train from London Bridge arrived at Preston Park, the ticket collector went to open the doors of the two first-class compartments. Naturally so. First-class service for first-class travellers. But when Mr Stark opened the smoker he was taken by surprise. Certainly not what he expected in a first-class compartment. For the man inside – a tall, skinny young fellow – was covered in blood. His face, his neck, his hands were crimsoned. Blood saturated his clothing, jacket, shirt front and trousers.

'I have been murderously attacked and fired at,' the young man told the ticket collector. 'Is there a doctor near?' Stark went into the carriage to help him down onto the platform. There were splashes of blood on the floor. And what appeared to be three gold coins but turned out to be cheap medals. The ticket collector picked them up. No, they didn't belong to him, the young man said. There was blood on the compartment's outer step, too.

Stark took the injured man into the ticket office and sat him down. His name, he said, was Arthur Lefroy.

'I am faint and want some water,' Lefroy told the ticket collector. He wanted a wash. He had had the most appalling experience. 'I have been fired at three times and struck on the head with a pistol,' Lefroy said. He had been knocked insensible.

But by whom? How could a man in an empty carriage have been set upon? There was no one there but Lefroy.

17

Another ticket collector at the scene pointed to a chain hanging out of the injured man's shoe. How on earth did a watch chain – for that is what it plainly was – find itself in a man's shoe? It was quite odd. Had the fellow attempted suicide? There was no other way in which his injuries could have been inflicted. But the watch and chain were his, Lefroy told his questioners who now included a policeman. He had put them in his shoe for safety.

It was thought best to send Lefroy on to Brighton, just ten minutes down the line. He could make a proper statement there about the attack he said that he had sustained and he could have proper medical treatment. That, in fact, was what the several witnesses thought he needed. And not just physical care. The man did seem odd.

Lefroy went first to Brighton Town Hall where he gave an account of what had happened. He lived in Wallington, he said, at 4 Cathcart Road. He had been to London earlier in the day and had caught the 2.10 pm train from London Bridge which stopped only at Preston Park and then Brighton. As a journalist, he was intending to interview Mrs Nye Chart, the celebrated owner of the Theatre Royal. The other occupants of the carriage had been a 'countryman' aged about 50 and an elderly man. Some time after leaving Croydon, Lefroy had heard a loud report and then knew nothing more until coming to as he neared Preston Park. He had found himself alone in a carriage awash with blood.

Lefroy had 13 shillings on him but another 20 shillings had been stolen, he said. Fortunately, he had secured his watch by placing it in his shoe. But what about the three gold 'coins' in his pocket? These matched those found on the floor of the compartment. Where they had come from he had no idea.

Lefroy's wounds were dressed at the County Hospital in Brighton. Though his neck was scratched he was not badly hurt. Would a man shot at such close quarters have got away so lightly? And furthermore, where were the attackers he had spoken of? Where were they supposed to have alighted? Did the countryman jump from the train? And did the old man escape in similar manner? Such questions must have occurred to the policeman, the ticket collectors, the medical staff. Of course they did, and each one seems to have discounted them for here in front of them was a man palpably deranged.

Hall, the surgeon, suggested that in view of what he had been through Lefroy ought to spend the night in hospital. No, impossible. 'I cannot stop the night as I have pressing business in London,' he said. 'I must be at my club by half past eight.' He was a member of the United Arts Club in the Strand. But he needed to go home to Wallington first.

It was on leaving hospital that Lefroy told Dr Hall and the ticket collector who had accompanied him that he had not much money. But, he said to them, 'I am shortly coming into a lot of property. If I have not money enough I will send it down and make it good. I will also make you two a handsome present.' They must have smiled to themselves at such an obviously lunatic promise.

It is much to the credit of railway employees, hospital staff and police that they endeavoured to take care of a man who had in some way perhaps hurt himself. So arrangements were made to ensure that he returned home to Wallington safely. And on the way back to Brighton station they even called at a haberdasher's so that he might buy a new celluloid collar to replace the one which had been torn off in the struggle.

On the train from London to Croydon his accompanying policeman, Sgt Holmes, on secondment from the Metropolitan Police, heard from a railway official that a man's body had been found on the line, near the entrance to Balcombe tunnel. He made no connection between that event and the man he was escorting but by the time they reached Croydon a telegram awaited Holmes. Has Lefroy a watch? If so, ask him its number. '56312,' Lefroy told the policeman but after inspection of the watch, he admitted his error. After all, how could one keep all these details in one's head? Especially after such an experience as he had gone through.

Holmes and Lefroy travelled from Croydon to Wallington by cab. The policeman delivered his charge to the very door before returning to Wallington station. Here another telegram awaited him. The man they had found on the railway line had no watch. And he had been subjected to a ferocious attack. It seemed that Lefroy had much to answer for. What about the watch that Lefroy had concealed in his shoe? Holmes was told to go back and check it out. The policeman went back to Cathcart Road but was reluctant to enter the house. After all, he realised, the man was most likely a murderer; he had undoubtedly killed the man flung out of the train at Balcombe. And so Holmes waited outside in the hope that he might arrest Lefroy in the street.

And then it was discovered that the bird had flown. He had changed his clothes, taken off his bandages, told the others in the house that he was going to his doctor and nipped out of the back entrance, leaving Holmes at the front.

MURDER.

£200 REWARD.

WHEREAS, on Monday, June 27th, ISAAC FREDERICK GOULD was murdered on the London Brighton and South Coast Railway, between Three Bridges and Balcombe, in East Sussex.

AND WHEREAS a Verdict of WILFUL MURDER has been returned by a Coroner's Jury against

PERCY LEFROY MAPLETON,

whose Portrait and Handwriting are given hereon, —

and who is described as being 22 years of age, height 5 ft. 8 or 9 in., very thin, hair (cut short) dark, small dark whiskers; dress, dark frock coat, and shoes, and supposed how black hat (worn at back of head), had scratches from fingers on throat, several wounds on head; the dressing of which involved the cutting of hair, recently lodged at 4, Cathcart Road, Wallington, was seen at 9.30 a.m. 24th ult., with his head bandaged, at the Fever Hospital, Liverpool Road, Islington. Had a gold open-faced watch (which he is likely to pledge). " Maker. Griffiths, Mile End Road, No. 16261."

One Half of the above Reward will be paid by Her Majesty's Government, and One Half by the Directors of the London Brighton and South Coast Railway, to any person (other than a person belonging to a Police Force in the United Kingdom) who shall give such information as shall lead to the discovery and apprehension of the said PERCY LEFROY MAPLETON, or others, the Murderer, or Murderers, upon his or their conviction; and the Secretary of State for the Home Department will advise the grant of Her Majesty's gracious PARDON to any accomplice, not being the person who actually committed the Murder, who shall give such evidence as shall lead to a like result.

Information to be given to the Chief Constable of East Sussex, Lewes, at any Police Station, or to

The Director of Criminal Investigations, Gt. Scotland Yard.

JULY 4th, 1881.

(4318)   Harrison and Sons, Printers in Ordinary to Her Majesty, St. Martin's Lane.

The 'wanted' notice for Lefroy which appeared in *The Daily Telegraph* – the first such notice to appear in a newspaper.

So who was this Arthur Lefroy whose escape embarrassed the police and aroused a perfect Lefroy mania as people sought to identify him from a drawing in *The Daily Telegraph*, the first instance of a public 'wanted' notice in the press?

At the time, he was living with the Claytons, relatives of his who ran a little boarding school for girls. Lefroy paid rent when he could. Certainly his relatives – Mrs Clayton was a half cousin – were tolerant of him. They had taken him into their home after he returned from Australia where he had been sent in the hope that the climate might help his frail constitution. He had gone with introductions to wealthy and influential people for the family was well connected. On both sides they occupied prominent positions in the services and the law. And there was money, too, in the family although Lefroy had spent his meagre £200 inheritance on the Australian venture. But within a year Lefroy was back in England and constantly in debt, never able to make ends meet and never able to find work. In consequence he had gained something of a reputation as a cadger of a few bob, a quid or two, from anyone who knew him. His shabby, down at heel appearance belied the middle class voice, the sometimes grand manner.

Perhaps it may be best to call the 22 year old Lefroy a failure for he had no success in anything he touched. He aimed at being a theatre critic and he had written a few notices about plays at the Brighton Theatre Royal, though Mrs Nye Chart did not know him and had not had an appointment with him as he claimed. He laid claim to being on the staff of the *Wallington and Carshalton Herald* for whom he wrote occasional, and most likely unpaid, pieces. Just before the tragedy in which he was so deeply mired he told relatives and friends that he had secured a post on *Era*, the theatrical newspaper. It was all wishful thinking. Recently the City of London Publishing Company had turned down his application for a post as had the *Newcastle Chronicle*. Nor was he, despite his claims, the writer of successful plays.

Lefroy was a fantasist, always lying, always, even his friends said, playing a part. Even the name which he had adopted since his return from Australia was his own concoction which he insisted that his friends and relatives use. No longer was he Percy Lefroy Mapleton. For the past 18 months he had been Arthur Lefroy, his private cards bearing that name and his letters that signature.

As with most judgements about people, opinions of him varied. Some friends thought him a 'shy, gentle, timid, good-natured boy'. Others saw him as 'a wretched, friendless lad . . . a miserable youth . . .'.

21

And with his departure from Wallington, the whole of England was alerted to this missing murderer. They sought a poor looking fish, a man with narrow sloping shoulders, a long thin neck, a sallow skin with a black moustache and a little tuft of dark whiskers at the side of the face.

Ports and railway stations were kept under observation. So too was the house at Wallington, his sister's house at Southend and all the other places where he might turn up. The government and the London, Brighton and South Coast Railway had each offered rewards of £100, equivalent today to about £4,500. For days there was no sign of the missing man though all over the country innocent males bearing the slightest resemblance to him were chased by mobs, hauled up before magistrates, accosted by aggressive strangers. But on 8th July, Francis Seale, another relative, who shared a room with Lefroy at Cathcart Road, received a telegram. It read: 'Please send my wages tonight without fail about eight o'clock.' It was sent by Lefroy from 32 Smith Street in Stepney where for a week he had hidden out, claiming to his landlady, Mrs Bickers, to be an engraver. Lefroy's hope was that in response to his coded message Seale would send him money. He intended to move on and presumably this is why he had in one of the drawers a false moustache and beard, both several shades lighter than his hair. Instead the police came to arrest him for the murder of Isaac Frederick Gold.

In the subsequent hearings before Cuckfield magistrates and later at Maidstone Assizes the whole bizarre tale came out.

Lefroy had joined the train at London Bridge, paying for his first-class ticket with his last few pence. A ticket collector on the platform recognised him as a man previously caught travelling without a ticket. The desperation of his financial situation is suggested by the pawn tickets for plated spoons; for a dress suit; for two pairs of trousers and jackets. And for a small revolver which he had that day redeemed for 5 shillings from a pawnbroker a couple of hundred yards from London Bridge. It was a weapon he had had in and out of hock several times that month. And to enable him to raise the money to redeem his pistol he had had to defraud the shop assistant of Mr Ellis, a Wallington tradesman, by a petty ruse that very morning. He had used fake coins of the kind found on the floor of the railway carriage. This quite unsubtle trick raised him 13s 4d.

At London Bridge, Lefroy entered the carriage occupied by a 64 year old coin dealer, Isaac Frederick Gold, who had been to London on business and was now returning by early afternoon train to his home at Preston Park. Not until they reached Merstham tunnel, some miles after the stop at Croydon, did Lefroy draw his revolver. In the adjoining carriage a witness heard four shots and mistook them for fog signals. There was something of a struggle after that for despite his years and a bullet wound in the neck, the old man was healthy and powerful enough to put up a fight. This was when Lefroy lost his collar and sustained some neck scratches. But he also had a knife which he used to frightening effect.

A stab wound in Gold's eye was large enough to admit a finger. His face, cut to the bone in places, bore a wound from the lobe of the right ear down the side of the lower jaw. The throat was cut and the muscles which form the floor of the mouth exposed. The wound continued up the left side of his face. A thumb was almost severed and his hands were cut as he had tried to protect himself. Gold could not long sustain the fight. Nor could his puny attacker. By the time they passed through Earlswood, half a dozen miles or so after the attack had begun, Gold was dead and his murderer composed enough to throw the pistol out of the window. One witness, living a hundred yards from the line at Horley, was to say that she thought she saw two men struggling in a compartment as the train passed through. If she saw anything, it could only have been Lefroy preparing the now dead Gold for his ultimate ejection from the train.

For the rest of the journey to Preston Park, Lefroy busied himself throwing out of the train items that would incriminate him. Thus Gold's and Lefroy's hats were found at Burgess Hill; Gold's purse at Hassocks Gate and his umbrella in Clayton tunnel; nearer yet to Preston Park, Lefroy's bloody collar was disposed of. And of course, Gold's body, the skull fractured in the fall, was hurled out of the door, leaving great gouts of blood on the step as it thudded to the ground at Balcombe tunnel. Had the ticket collectors inspected the compartment more carefully when first they met Lefroy, doubtless their conclusions might have been different for they would have seen bullet holes in the seat cushions and panelling. And possibly they would have wondered too about the cheap medals on the carriage floor which were disowned by Lefroy. Why had the so-called attackers not made off with them? Perhaps under pressure Lefroy might have admitted that it was with some of these spurious coins that he had that morning tricked Mr Ellis's lad of 13s 4d.

Percy Lefroy Mapleton had the distinction of being the first British-born railway murderer. In fact in 1864, Franz Muller, a German, committed the first murder on a British train. But it is a petty distinction for a petty young man.

In court Lefroy sported a new silk top hat and a buttoned up black frock coat. He was quite the dandy, adjusting his profile for the benefit of the court artists. He was, said Montague Williams QC who defended him so ably, 'a man steeped in a kind of petty, strutting, theatrical vanity'. At the end of the trial Lefroy was to thank the jury for their careful consideration of the case but after being pronounced guilty could not resist declaring in a theatrical voice: 'Some day you will learn, when too late, that you have murdered me'.

The apparently motiveless murder of Frederick Gold had been carried out by a deeply disturbed man. However despite petitions to the Home Secretary and pleas not to execute him, Percy Lefroy Mapleton was hanged at Lewes on 29th November 1881.

3

SURREY
PASTORALE

The Murder of an Unknown Man at Blindley Heath,
July 1910

In 1910, Crippen's year, Blindley
Heath had its own murder. It was a pretty nasty, brutal affair but they
never found anyone for it so there was not much of a story for the
national press. The man in the barn was just as dead as Belle Elmore,
the little doctor's wife, but his fate didn't have quite the pulling power.
The murder at Blindley Heath, that swampy old place where
commoners' ancient grazing rights were still observed, caused little
stir beyond the locality. 'It is needless to say that the terrible discovery
has caused a great sensation in the Blindley Heath district,' the *Surrey
Mirror* announced as if to say nowhere else was much exercised by the
event.

Down the years the crime had its local resonances. The gangs of
itinerant haymakers and harvesters refused to sleep on the straw and
sacks in the barn where the outrage had occurred. Nor would they ever
speak of it to outsiders. Nor would you hear much about it at Gibbs'
Store or even at The Blue Anchor. The village remained silent on the
matter. Twenty and thirty years later, young farm lads expressing
curiosity about the murder at Stanton Hall Farm, would be told to shut
up, to get on with their work. It was as if the murderer were still alive
and living thereabouts. As if everybody knew the truth of it but nobody
was saying.

But perhaps the most interesting feature of this relatively minor case
is that it offers an example of an innocent man saved by an overriding
desire for justice on the part of magistrates and the Grand Jury. Or
against that, does it show a consummate failure to examine thoroughly

The Blue Anchor pub at Blindley Heath.

the facts behind the barn murder at Blindley Heath? It is difficult to filter out from the thin documentation what precisely happened on that summer Sunday night. But it is worth a try.

At about five o'clock on Monday morning, 18th July 1910, the body of a man was found in the cattle shed attached to Holland's Barn in Hare Lane. The victim, aged between 60 and 65, had injuries to the head, arms and legs. There was a Y-shaped wound to his forehead and severe bruising to the left eye. The left ear was badly cut. His nose was broken, his cheeks fractured in two places. Doctor Morehead conducting the post mortem thought that fists alone could not have accounted for the nine fractured ribs. In his view the victim had been jumped upon. He suggested that other wounds were inflicted by a blunt instrument. No particular injury had caused the man's death, said Dr Morehead. He had died from shock from the number of injuries he had suffered.

This elderly man, unknown in the area, was assumed to be a tramp, one of those who moved from one workhouse Casual Ward to another in the course of his wanderings, the sort of vagrant who in summer slept in barns rather than in the 'spikes'.

The tramp – and let us stick with the assumption that that is what he was – was a small man, 5'3" in height, toothless, sandy-haired. Both of his feet were deformed and he would have walked with short steps. No one locally could bring to mind such a distinctive figure. A heart was tattooed on his left breast. He wore cord trousers and a shirt but no stockings, boots or coat. It was never established what became of these. His sole possessions were a broken table knife and a few coppers.

Mrs Isabella Coomber, seemingly an itinerant summer field-worker, who found the body lying half outside the shed 'covered in blood', explained to the Coroner's jury and later in the Oxted Magistrates Court, that she had been given permission to sleep in the barn by William Jupp who farmed Stanton Hall. She had gone there on the previous evening at about 10 pm but had found the old man there. She decided to move to another barn about a mile away. The next morning when she went up the lane she saw the body. But over the months she was to deny in court that she was actually in the shed when the tramp and James Kemp, his common law wife Mrs Proudley and her 25 year old son, Frank, also known as Kemp, came in together. Mrs Coomber also denied telling another witness that a quarrel had broken out before she left. No, she had not been threatened by the Kemps that if she did not keep quiet ...

Mrs Coomber insisted that she had heard nothing all night. She had been sleeping a mile away down the road. Anyway, if there had been a disturbance in the lane nobody would have taken much notice at this time of the year, what with so many itinerants and gypsies in the neighbourhood. Summertime, there were always rows.

After finding the body, she had left the barn and had met James Kemp and Mrs Proudley in the lane. Mrs Coomber told them about the body. But it all sounds fishy – what were they all up to at five o'clock in the morning? Together they had gone to Jupp's farmhouse. William Jupp and his son, along with Mrs Coomber and Kemp, had then gone to see the body after which they had sent for the doctor and the police.

By the Monday morning a description of a man being sought by the police was circulated through Surrey and the adjacent counties. Oddly, no name was yet given. The wanted man was described as 5'10" tall, with a black eye and a scar on the back of his right hand. He was in his mid-twenties and clean shaven. He was wearing a dirty, white slop (a frock-smock), common among countrymen until the First World War. On the Sunday evening he had been seen at The Blue Anchor in Blindley Heath.

On Tuesday night, 19th July, Albert Baggs, a general labourer, was arrested at Handcross by Police Sergeant Huntley. He was taken to Haywards Heath police station. His clothing was taken from him for forensic examination.

There was some satisfaction at such prompt police alertness. Here was a man with a badly discoloured eye and a cut on his face. Furthermore, there were bloodstains on his jacket and trousers. He matched perfectly the wanted man's description. At Oxted Magistrates Court, he explained that he had been in a fight on the Saturday night. 'I had a punch on the nose and the face,' he said, 'and I had no pocket handkerchief.' Two weeks later, he was discharged.

The police now had another suspect, Frank Kemp, but he was nowhere to be found. The Coroner demanded strenuous efforts to get him into court. But he did not respond to the summons to attend the inquest on 2nd August. Where was he?

At least there was some temporary consolation. At the inquest in the Forman Village Institute, the Deputy Coroner announced that the body had now been identified as that of Albert Pinch, a 72 year old farm labourer. He travelled round Surrey and Kent, moving on from place to place and occasionally returning to Tunbridge Wells where his even older step-mother, Mrs Twort, lived. The police had taken her a photograph of the murdered man. Ah yes, she recognised him at once. Yes, she knew that nose: he was so like his father. And yes, he had a tattoo on his left breast. A heart. And the cap, yes, she'd washed that for Albert last time he was home.

Then who should turn up at his Tunbridge Wells home but the said Albert Pinch? He had been on the tramp for two months but finding work hard to come by had returned 'in exceptionally good health'. Not surprisingly, Pinch was amazed to hear the news of his murder. 'I have been away of late on farms,' he said, 'and I never saw the newspapers so that I did not know at all what had happened to me.'

The Coroner adjourned the inquest on 2nd August for 14 days when Kemp did not answer the summons and there was a further adjournment on 16th August as he had still not been found. Then there was some progress. Frank Kemp was arrested at Peasmarsh on Monday, 12th September. He appeared the following day at the resumed inquest. Questioned about his failure to answer to the earlier summons, Kemp explained that on that occasion he had been drinking, had fallen asleep and had awakened too late. He knew nothing of the second hearing, he said, until his arrest, when he had tried to convince the arresting officer that his name was William Foreman.

Kemp had been following the traditional route of an unskilled, casual farm labourer. When he left his employment at Old Lodge Farm in Dormansland without warning on the Monday night or the Tuesday

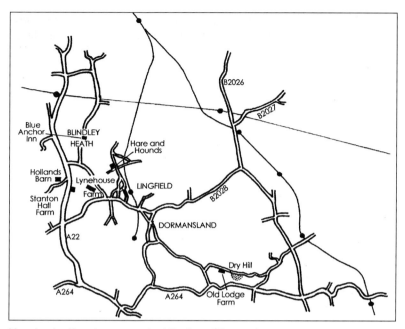

Map showing Kemp's movements at the time of the murder.

morning after the murder he had gone to Smart's Hill, Penshurst and Goudhurst. At Wadhurst he had been taken on for nine days' haymaking. Then he had returned to Goudhurst, Tunbridge Wells, again to Smarts Hill and Blindley Heath. On hearing that he was too late to attend the inquest he had gone to Little Common, Romney Marsh and Peasmarsh. He stayed there till the Monday when he was arrested.

There were two important factors which ought to have been resolved and which never were. The first related to Kemp's movements on the evening of Sunday 17th July and the morning of the next day. The second was whether he wore bloodstained clothing. In the several hearings at which Frank Kemp appeared, these matters were not pursued resolutely enough.

In the week before the murder Kemp had been working for Mr Henry Anstee at Old Lodge Farm. Like many casual workers, he was accommodated in a shed. Kemp had left the farm at 6.30 pm on the Saturday after receiving his week's wages of 17s 6d. Anstee did not see him again until 8.45 am on the Monday.

On the Sunday, at about 6.30 pm, Kemp was seen at The Hare and

Hounds, Lingfield, with old James Kemp and Mrs Proudley. They had sat drinking outside the public house and left after an hour or so.

Later, Kemp had turned up at The Blue Anchor in Blindley Heath. At about ten o'clock, he had walked part of the way home with Joseph Jones, a caravan dweller. Jones agreed that Kemp had walked off towards Lingfield, he assumed to Old Lodge Farm. But what if the drunken Frank Kemp had cut off to the right, down Hare Lane, where he met up once more with James Kemp and Mrs Proudley? What if at the barn they had met the tramp and the quarrel such as Mrs Coomber had denied had broken out? What if then . . .?

Kemp told the court that he had returned to Old Lodge Farm and that the shed where he slept had been locked. He said he had climbed in over the top of the door. He had lain down in the straw on some sacks beside the manger, sleeping as usual in one large sack. The next morning he rose at about five o'clock. He 'just walked about for a time'.

However, according to James Berringer, a cowman at Lyne House Farm, at about 6.45 am on the Monday, a tall young man, dark complexioned, hurried through the farmyard on the way to Lingfield. He wore a dirty white slop. He had bloodstains on one hand. Berringer called to him to stop, believing him to be trespassing. But the man ignored him. In court Berringer pointed out Kemp as the trespasser. He had come across the fields from the direction of Holland's Barn.

At about seven o'clock Kemp called in at The Hare and Hounds at Lingfield and had two pints of shandy gaff and a couple of buns. The landlord, William Istead, recognised him. He had known Kemp for years. Albert Boorer, a labourer, also confirmed that Kemp was there.

Times, of course, are inevitably approximate. It would not have been impossible for Kemp to have crossed Lyne House Farm and to have been at The Hare and Hounds in the early hours. At some time that morning, too, he called in at Mrs Lacey's store at Dormansland. There is nothing inconsistent in this either. But what was he doing in the Blindley Heath area at that hour? And had he slept that Sunday night at Old Lodge Farm?

Marsh, the foreman at Old Lodge Farm, had looked in the barn at five o'clock on the Monday morning, checking that Kemp was there for work because labourers, after being paid, frequently left without warning. No sign of Kemp, he said, and the sack he usually slept inside was not on the straw. It was in the same position on the Monday morning as it was on Saturday afternoon. Marsh believed that Kemp had not been back on the Sunday.

Kemp, of course, claimed that he had got up at about five o'clock and 'just walked about for a time.' As a matter of fact, he said, he had been in Holme Lane Field at 6 am but he hadn't seen anyone. But was he telling the truth?

There are certainly suspicious gaps in the accounts of Kemp's movements.

Then there was the matter of Kemp's clothing. Berringer had seen a man passing through the farmyard wearing a slop. He identified Kemp. And Albert Boorer, in The Hare and Hounds that morning with Kemp, was certain that his slop was bloodstained. When that same Monday morning, Kemp harnessed up the horse and took it down to Lingfield station, both Henry Long and George Grevett, carting cement there, remembered seeing his bloodstained slop.

So what was Kemp's story, the Coroner asked him. What had he been wearing on the Monday morning? A light cloth coat and cord trousers, Kemp replied, and definitely not a slop. Were these not Marsh, the foreman's belongings, clothes that he had left in the barn, he was asked. He said they were not. Well, how long had he had the cords, the Coroner asked. A fortnight, Kemp answered. He'd got them in Sevenoaks. So where were these clothes now? He had worn them out, was the answer. He had thrown away the trousers at Little Common near Bexhill and the jacket at Battle. The trousers he was wearing now had been given to him by a man working for Mr Jackman between Little Common and Pevensey Marsh. The jacket he had on he had had from a labouring man at Squirrel Lane in Battle. Plausible enough in the poor community of casual workers where exchange of goods was easier than the exchange of money.

Kemp was also questioned about some clothes burnt at Dry Hill, no more than a half mile from his workplace, on the Monday. Hadn't somebody at Dry Hill questioned him on this? But the importance of this crucial question seems to have been lost.

Is the truth of Kemp's clothing that he wore the slop at work and later burnt it when he realised that it had blood on it? Had he then taken off in Marsh's clothes?

At the inquest the Coroner was certain that Mrs Coomber had not told all she knew. Why had she gone back to the barn so early in the morning? Did she have intimations that there had been something seriously amiss the previous night? Calling her back, the Coroner invited her to take the opportunity to tell the truth. But she would have none of it. 'I have told you all I know,' she said.

31

The inquest then returned a verdict of 'Wilful Murder' against Frank Kemp in his real name, Henry Francis Smith.

In September, Kemp, dressed in 'somewhat ragged clothing', and now charged with murder, made three appearances before the magistrates at Oxted. At their fourth sitting the magistrates expressed their view that the evidence did not justify committing the accused for trial. Really?

Then came the insistence of the DPP that this was an unsatisfactory conclusion and that the case must be presented to the Grand Jury. A bill of indictment was prepared against Kemp. Certainly, at Guildford Assizes in November Mr Justice Grantham felt that more careful investigation was required. But in turn, following the example of the magistrates, the Grand Jury threw out the indictment. A verdict of Not Guilty was returned and Kemp was discharged.

Was an innocent man saved by a desire for justice on the part of magistrates and the Grand Jury? Was there just not enough evidence to make it reasonable to proceed against Kemp? Or were the circumstances just not satisfactorily investigated and a guilty man walked free?

Whatever the answer, it is easy to understand the stir it caused in Blindley Heath – and perhaps why the people there were always disinclined to talk about it.

4

LIKE
TWO BROTHERS

The Murder of Eric Tombe at Kenley,
April 1922

Common enough, conmen. And some of them are very persuasive, dangerously so. And they give such an air of confidence. Like the smartly dressed chap just finishing lunch at the Bar Hotel in Scarborough. At first sight no one would have taken him for a rogue who had tricked several businessmen in various parts of the country. He had been to Hereford and Cheltenham and gone off with his wallet bulging. And up north, in 20 or so places, he had also done very well. It was a simple enough strategy. He placed advertisements in local newspapers – 'employment with outstanding prospects; small financial investment required'. No references required either, just a cash deposit in lieu. And our conman simply waited for the money to roll in and then it was off to some other place, as Fitzsimmons as he was calling himself here in Scarborough, or perhaps Williams or Tongs or Tombe or one of the other names that took his fancy.

But in November 1922 Inspector Abbott of the Scarborough force had had his attention drawn to Mr James Fitzsimmons who claimed to be the son of a wealthy Carlisle magistrate. The policeman had decided to pay him a visit that lunch time. So with two other detectives Abbott went into the dining room. Mr Fitzsimmons? Might they have a word? About the agency he was running? Of course, the young man replied, he would gladly answer any questions. Perhaps he would be allowed to get some papers from his room. They would explain everything. Most certainly, Inspector Abbott agreed, and the officers would accompany him. It was as they climbed the stairs that Fitzsimmons suddenly reached in his pocket and drew a revolver. As the officers struggled to disarm him, there was a shot and their quarry slumped to the ground. In minutes he was dead.

A search of the dead man's room revealed a number of interesting items. There was a croupier's eyeshade, a mask, a toy revolver, an automatic pistol, a suitcase initialled ET, a passport in the name of Tongs, war medals, army discharge papers, some documents relating to someone called Eric Tombe and 200 blank cheques, each one with a pencilled signature, also Eric Tombe. And Fitzsimmons turned out to be called Ernest Dyer, a man 'known to the Metropolitan police.'

The event caused little stir outside Scarborough. Remarkable though that no one saw fit to approach Lloyd's Bank about the cheque book bearing the name Eric Tombe or to chase whatever other information there was in the documents bearing this man's name. As it was, the death of Ernest Dyer, aka James Fitzsimmons, passed off without much follow-up.

It was ten months later when a retired clergyman, the Rev Mr Gordon Tombe, anxious that for over a year, since April 1922, he and his wife had heard nothing of their son, went to Scotland Yard with his worries. He explained to Superintendent Francis Carlin how he had himself endeavoured to find Eric but the matter had assumed some quite alarming features. The fact of the matter was that Mr Tombe feared that something dreadful had befallen his son. Could he be dead?

Senior police officers are not infrequently faced with such dilemmas. And not infrequently they are able to persuade worried parents or husbands or lovers that the likelihood is that the persons whose lives they are fearful for have disappeared of their own volition. Perhaps most reports of missing persons do not merit much expenditure of police time. Either the missing person will turn up or continue to lie low.

But on that September day in 1923 Superintendent Carlin heard out the clergyman's story and believed that some investigation was necessary. Especially as, until the previous November, he had been involved in the search for the confidence trickster, Ernest Dyer. And this was a name which Mr Tombe had mentioned. The clergyman had found out only recently that Dyer had been his son's partner in a horse stud. He had discovered this when making enquiries about Eric's whereabouts. Dyer had obviously been defrauding his son, he told the policeman. But Dyer was dead, Carlin was able to tell the clergyman. Dyer had been shot in Scarborough last November.

At this point Francis Carlin and Gordon Tombe were able to piece

The Welcomes stables at Kenley.

together the relationship of the two young men who had met in the last months of the war as army officers posted to the Air Ministry. When the war was over they had teamed up together in business. They both had army gratuities and Dyer, an inveterate gambler, had increased his by winning a huge sum on the Lincoln Handicap. They had first of all invested in an unsuccessful motor engineering garage. Then they raked up enough to invest in The Welcomes stud at Kenley. This was a going venture when they took it over in 1920 with 20 horses in the stables. Tombe was running another motor engineering workshop in Harlesden where he lived for most of the time. In effect, he was a sleeping partner as far as The Welcomes was concerned and whilst he paid regular visits to the stud, he never stayed there. Dyer and his wife and three children lived in the house at The Welcomes. At the time, despite the ups and downs of their business ventures, the two men appeared to be staunch friends. Indeed, as one witness was to say, they were like two brothers.

But Dyer was more inclined to living the high life than working to make the stud a success. Drink, gambling, other women were major interests and the promise that The Welcomes had held out soon dissipated. His personal finances were in turmoil. In April 1921 a fire destroyed many of the buildings and several horses died. The suspicious insurance company refused to pay a penny. Eric Tombe, still solvent with his other business interests intact, probably had some pertinent queries too for he was not likely to have attempted such a risky measure. Dyer's financial situation was parlous now. Then, in April 1922, it seems that the partnership was dissolved. Dyer's subsequent fate was known but, asked the clergyman, where was his son?

Mr Tombe told Carlin how he had placed notices in the newspapers asking Eric to come forward. But there had been no reply. He had scoured his son's haunts in London. By one stroke of luck, he had recalled that Eric went regularly to a particular hairdresser in the Haymarket. It suggests how desperate for information he was that such a straw was grabbed at. And remarkably, the hairdresser was able to recall Eric Tombe, even had his address in the appointments book. Of course, didn't he have some horse business, stables, a stud, something like that? The Rev Mr Tombe was surprised to hear of The Welcomes Stud Farm in Hayes Lane at Kenley, south of Croydon. Nor had he ever heard of Eric's partner, Ernest Dyer. But he determined to go down there and have a word. Surely they would have some information.

The Welcomes Stud Farm – the name sounded pretty impressive. But when he arrived there old Mr Tombe was in for a shock. The place was a wreck. The buildings had been gutted by fire and the paddock and the grounds were deserted and overgrown. But Mrs Watson, Dyer's mother in law, was living there in a cottage. She could give him little information but she understood that Eric Tombe had gone abroad though she couldn't say where.

It was after the visit to Kenley and after further discussions with his distraught wife at their Sydenham home that Mr Tombe decided to visit his son's bank, Lloyd's in Bond Street. There he heard a story that concerned him even more. It seemed that Eric's substantial account had been systematically robbed. It was this discovery which persuaded the alarmed Mr Tombe that the whole matter was becoming too complex for him to resolve. He needed help now and it was for that reason that he had gone to Scotland Yard. And the mention of Dyer's name had made Superintendent Carlin determined to disentangle the mystery.

Carlin's visit to the Bond Street bank confirmed all that the elderly clergyman had told him. The bank manager explained that young Mr Tombe had called twice to arrange the transfer of some of his money to an account in Paris and had made a further arrangement for his partner to be joint account holder. No, he hadn't been sure what Eric Tombe looked like, he said. Carlin surmised that it had been Dyer up to his tricks.

Over several months, the bank manager said, there had been

Ernest Dyer.

confirmatory letters and cheques withdrawing the money although there had been no transactions of any kind for well over a year. The manager explained that the account had been reduced from £2,570 and that in April 1922 a sum of £1,350 had gone to the Paris account marked 'for the use of Ernest Dyer'. A letter dated 24th April purporting to come from Eric Tombe requested that Dyer be allowed to draw on the Paris account. Another letter of July 1922 gave Ernest Dyer power of attorney allowing him to draw freely on the Bond Street account. There was also a letter in the bank files. 'Dear Mrs Dyer,' it said, 'I enclose you a cheque for £60, being the winding up of poor Bill's (Ernest Dyer's) affairs. Yours sincerely, Eric Gordon Tombe.'

It was at about this time that a young woman had called on the manager, expressing her fears that Eric Tombe's money was being siphoned off by Dyer, and she had confirmed that the signatures on several documents were not in his hand. Finally the account had run dry even though a number of dud cheques were presented in the West Country.

Through the bank Carlin was able to trace the girl who had been suspicious of Dyer. They had been great friends at one time, Dyer and Tombe and the young woman who, incidentally, was never publicly identified. But she had not seen either man for the past 18 months. In fact, she recalled that they had all been due to go off to Paris for a week-end in late April 1922. Another girl was going with them. (What Dyer's wife had to say about this is not clear but he was always elusive.) They knew they'd have a great time, especially with Bill, the name by which Dyer was known to his friends. He was full of fun. And he was such a spender. But on the day they were due to take off, Dyer had turned up very flustered. Sorry, he had said, it's off. We can't go to Paris. Eric had apparently received a telegram asking him to an important business meeting somewhere abroad. The young woman remembered how tense and worried Bill had seemed that day. Carlin had asked her further questions. Where was he now? She didn't know. Up north, she thought, but she couldn't be certain.

Some time later – it must have been in the early summer of 1922 – the girl had talked again to Dyer about Eric Tombe and the fact that he had sent her no word of what he was up to. He just seemed to have disappeared. Dyer had answered that after their joint venture at The Welcomes had foundered Eric had simply decided to dissolve the partnership and had gone off. In fact, on the very day that decision had been reached, Dyer claimed he had driven Tombe to Croydon where

Eric Tombe.

he understood that he was intending to catch a bus to London. He had not seen him since, he said.

There was something about this tale or about Dyer's unconvincing manner that concerned the young woman. She had expressed her dissatisfaction and even suggested that she might go to the police. If she did that, Dyer told her, he might as well blow out his brains. So she didn't go to the police. But she did go to the bank warning the manager of her doubts about the Tombe account.

Carlin traced another young woman who said that she was Tombe's fiancee. Dyer had also told her about taking his former partner to Croydon. The last time she had spoken to Dyer he had cut off their telephone conversation when she had persisted with her questions. Like Eric Tombe, Ernest 'Bill' Dyer had then just disappeared from her life.

At least there was little difficulty in establishing the date of Tombe's disappearance. It was about 19th April 1922 when Eric Tombe had visited his parents' house in Sydenham. They had been out but other relatives were able to say that on that day they had seen him. And it was before 25th April 1922, the day on which the trip to Paris with the girls had been called off. The best estimate of Tombe's disappearance was 21st April.

But had Eric Tombe simply disappeared? Bearing in mind that Dyer had carried a gun in Scarborough nearly a year earlier, Carlin wondered if a murder might have been committed. But where? And how?

Much has been made of Mrs Tombe's dreams in resolving the puzzle. It is said that she had terrible nightmares in which Eric was dead. And every time, she dreamt of his being buried under a heavy stone slab on a farm. It is more likely, however, that an experienced officer like Carlin would think it reasonable to search The Welcomes just in case the answer to the questions of Eric Tombe's fate might be found there.

On 12th September 1923 Superintendent Carlin, joined by Detective Inspector Hedges, the local man who some years later was to investigate the notorious Croydon poisoning case, went to The Welcomes. With them was a party of constables who were to search the premises. As the Rev Mr Tombe had said, the place was practically derelict, simply a gloomy shell, abandoned, neglected and sad. Crumbling paths, weeds and untended grass in the paddocks added to an overpowering air of decay. Despite this, Dyer's in-laws and his three children still lived in the cottage.

The policemen searched the buildings diligently and found nothing. But Carlin remained convinced that what he was seeking was somewhere here. He instituted a search of the cesspits on the edge of the paddock. In the course of the day and well into the night, working eventually by the light of oil lamps, they moved several hundredweight of cement, loose bricks and rubble from the filled-in cesspits. Then the men worked in the water collected at the bottom. It was exhausting work. Dispiriting, too, when the first cesspit yielded nothing. Nor did the second. Nor the third. But late at night their hard labour was rewarded. Right at the bottom of the fourth cesspit, in an arched recess, was a body, still clothed, with a muffler round the neck. The corpse, wrapped in an overcoat, was in a fair state of preservation. And there were items – tie pin, cuff links, gold wrist watch – that the distressed old clergyman was later to identify.

It was Eric Tombe's body. His skull was shattered. He had been shot in the back of the head. The Coroner's jury did not hesitate to bring in a verdict of 'Wilful murder' by Ernest Dyer.

Mrs Dyer, a much put-upon wife, very much at her husband's every command, recalled that in the summer of 1922, fearing to meet his creditors, he had disappeared. He was of course at that time carrying out the frauds which were to lead to his shooting in Scarborough. One night Mrs Dyer had been roused by a strange sound in the paddock. It was as if bucket loads of stones were being thrown down a drain. When she went to investigate, she had been surprised to find her husband there. In the dark, he was filling in the cesspit with bricks and rubble. He had sent her off to the house muttering the usual explanation that because of his creditors he could only come there under cover of darkness. She did not follow up by questioning what it was that he was actually doing there at that time of night.

But what an ill-starred couple, Tombe and Dyer. A waster and possibly an innocent. Yet both ended up dead, both very young. Tombe only 29; Dyer a couple of years older. Both intelligent, lively men. But one of them was ruthless and when he feared that his partner, still with plenty of cash, was leaving him, he had had no hesitation in shooting him. Yet the same man need not have hastened his own death. When Detective Inspector Abbott approached him that day in a Scarborough hotel, there was no need for him to react as he did. They were out to question him about fraud. Did Ernest Dyer think he was to be arrested for murder? Is that why he drew his gun? Was it that mistake which led to his death just after lunch?

Yet Mrs Watson, musing on the affair, and seemingly not quite understanding her son-in-law's calculating nature, was to say of Dyer and Tombe that they had been like two brothers.

Cain and Abel perhaps?

5

A VERY
RESPECTABLE SUBURBAN FAMILY

The Murders of Edmund Duff, Vera Sidney and Violet
Sidney at Croydon,
April 1928; February 1929; March 1929

This is South Croydon in the 1920s.
And here are South Park Hill Road and Birdhurst Rise, just off Coombe
Road, a highly respectable part of Croydon. The genteel inhabitants
here for the most part range from the quite comfortable to the
decidedly wealthy. You might say it is a prim and proper part of town
and that behind their lace curtains they are steady reliable folk. You
don't normally have people breaking the law hereabouts and you
certainly don't have them committing murder. Certainly not in the late
1920s. In these solid Victorian and Edwardian houses, you have
professional people, people of substance. They employ maids and
cooks; they have telephones and motor cars; they belong to clubs and
societies and they play golf and bridge. The careers of the gentlemen as
bankers and auctioneers, solicitors and accountants, bring them into
contact with other people of significance, people like themselves.

Here at 29 Birdhurst Rise lived Violet Sidney with her daughter, 40
year old Vera, in a large detached house, on the outside solid, rather
forbidding, and inside, like many others of the neighbouring
residences, dark, a place of shadows. And not far away, only minutes
on foot, at 16 South Park Hill Road, her daughter Grace with her
husband, Edmund Duff, and their three children, had their home, Hurst
Rise. At Number 6 in the same road, living only a short step away with
his wife and two children, was Grace's 38 year old brother, Tom, a
successful professional entertainer. And though the Duffs rarely visited

43

Tom, they met frequently enough at Violet's house for they visited the old lady nearly every day.

Of course, for some in this genteel quarter there was the problem of keeping up appearances. Edmund Duff, for example, had worked in Africa for the Colonial Office. The fact was, however, that his pension was not adequate for he had never occupied a very significant position and once back in England he had had to take on a quite modest clerical post. And sadly he was not a good manager of what money he had. From time to time, he sold when he should buy, bought when he should sell. His assets diminished by the year; in total a sum of £5,000 was frittered away. Inevitably, Edmund and Grace Duff were dependent on Mrs Sidney and her other daughter, Vera, for handouts, including their son, Johnny's, school fees. Now, they were even unable to keep a full-time maid and were making do with an afternoons-only girl. The shame of it. And it was not as if Edmund was a young man. He was 59 after all. Was he some day going to leave Grace, 17 years his junior, impoverished?

And then unexpectedly he died.

On Monday 23rd April 1928, before he went on a visit to Hampshire to do a spot of fishing with a friend, Edmund called in at his doctor's. He had severe abdominal pain and diarrhoea but Dr Binning gave him something and off he went. He felt passably well on the Tuesday but on the next day he was feverish, attributing this to a recurrence of malaria. On Friday 27th April, he came home by train feeling decidedly peaky. Even so, he took supper, a meal of chicken, potatoes, peas, but he picked at his plate and ate little. He drank his usual bottle of Bass but before long he was ill. Dr Elwell, Binning's partner, was called. He sent the sick man to bed, prescribing quinine and aspirin for what he called acute food poisoning.

The next day Edmund's condition worsened and there was constant vomiting and diarrhoea. His temperature fell sharply and he had severe cramps in the stomach and feet. Despite the ministrations of both Drs Elwell and Binning, in the evening of 28th April, Edmund Duff died in the most appalling agony.

The doctors were puzzled. Edmund was a robust man. He should not have succumbed so easily to food poisoning. Unable to issue a death certificate, they put the matter in the hands of the coroner who ordered a post mortem and inquest. Some days later, there being nothing untoward according to the analyst, the inquest jury brought in a verdict of death from natural causes.

In the next few months, though she was not greatly better off, with the insurance money and possibly with a little further financial support from her mother Violet and younger sister Vera, Grace Duff moved from the house that she and her husband had rented in South Park Hill Road to a leasehold property, 59 Birdhurst Rise. Now Grace, a most handsome woman, slender, dark haired, with wide open, slate-blue eyes, had come to live even closer to her mother and sister.

It was in early January of the following year that Vera began to record in her diary how poorly she was feeling. She was exhausted; she felt sick. Unusual for her, for she was a healthy woman. She was a golfer and a bridge player and had a good circle of friends and was often seen about in her small motor car. And now suddenly she was listless, feeling completely out of sorts.

On Monday 11th February, Vera took supper with her mother. It had been prepared by the cook, Kate Noakes. There was vegetable soup for Vera – her mother rarely touched the stuff – and then there was fish, fried potatoes and pudding and fruit. Almost immediately after the meal, Vera began vomiting and this continued throughout the night. The following day she could eat nothing, existing on tea and Oxo. On 13th February, when her aunt, Mrs Greenwell, came to visit, Vera, feeling slightly better, came downstairs for lunch. This time there was a thick brown soup, that old favourite of the pre-war English dinner table, chicken with parsley sauce, potatoes and sprouts followed by stewed pears and baked custard.

Once again, Vera was ill, vomiting violently. Dr Elwell was sent for. So severe was the pain that when he was summoned in the early hours of 14th February he gave her a morphine injection. He and Dr Binning now decided to call in a specialist for they were mystified by the symptoms. It did not seem like food poisoning, they thought, because the temperature was extremely high. Only gastric flu, said the specialist.

But early on Friday, 15th February 1929, Vera Sidney died. The doctors, confident in the specialist's assessment, saw no cause not to issue a death certificate. With hindsight they were probably to put a different construction on matters for on the same day that Vera had had her first bout of sickness, Mrs Noakes and the cat had taken some of the soup and both had been violently ill. As it was, Vera was buried with little curiosity about the circumstances.

The 68 year old Violet was shattered by the death of her favourite daughter. Now, despite the fact that Grace was only doors away and her son Tom living in South Park Hill Road within a five minute walk, she felt the absence of Vera acutely. She must have felt that her world was caving in with the loss of such a loyal companion who must have eased the emotional pain of her past. Had Violet ever recovered from the humiliation of her husband's desertion? That had happened years earlier, in 1891, when she was only 31. The scoundrel, he had left her for another woman who had had a child by him. Since then, although a successful barrister with a London practice, he had made little contribution to the family. Perhaps just sometimes the anger and self-pity surged up. Even a long-standing, long-distance romantic attachment with a Frenchman had been no more than an exchange of love poems written in French. And in 1928 he too had died. Vera's dependable support over the years was surely going to be missed.

Run down and tearful, Violet had the doctor in to see her. On 25th February he prescribed a tonic, Metatone. Over the next few days Violet seemed to pull herself together. At lunch time on the 5th March, she took her usual dose of the tonic, pouring the last dregs of the bottle into a wine glass of water. At once she declared that she had been poisoned, the liquid had tasted so nasty and gritty, and this was what she told Dr Binning. She would not, however, say who it was that she suspected. Again the doctor came to the conclusion that his patient was suffering from food poisoning. But Violet Sidney's upset was more than that. Her symptoms were not dissimilar to those exhibited by her son-in-law who had died the previous year and they also bore some resemblance to those of her beloved daughter who had died not three weeks earlier. But death came more swiftly in Violet's case. Within six hours of taking the lunchtime dose of Metatone, she was dead. Like Edmund and Vera she had died in excruciating agony.

Dr Binning, unsure now of the cause of Violet's death, referred the matter to the coroner. Certain organs were removed from the body for analysis. The analysts discovered evidence of arsenic in the body and also at the bottom of the Metatone bottle. By the time the report was made available to the coroner, however, Violet had been buried. Ten days later she was exhumed. There followed the exhumation of Vera and Edmund. Both bodies contained liberal amounts of arsenic. The writer Richard Whittington-Egan colourfully describes Edmund as 'stuffed to the gunnels with arsenic.'

Over the next several weeks three separate, lengthy and complicated inquests took place. Family and friends gave their versions of events though inevitably these did not always tally; maids and cooks asserted the devotedness of the Duffs; doctors were at times confused and

Edmund Duff, victim number one.

Vera Sidney, victim number two.

Violet Sidney, victim number three.

47

analysts and mortuary attendants under some pressure. How had Edmund looked? Where was the poison kept? Was Tom at his mother's house on the day she died? When was the soup made? Was Tom's wife on good terms with her sister in law? Was there a paper seal on the beer bottle? Had young John any idea of how his father came to be poisoned? What was the colour of the organs? Questions, questions, questions at nine inquest sittings between 8th March and 31st July to determine Violet's death; another nine sittings between 22nd March and 20th July for Vera; eight more sittings in Edmund's case between 5th July and 6th August. And practically the same stage-army every time. Grace, Tom, Mrs Noakes, doctors, analysts, maids and the whole complex rigmarole of investigation.

Edmund's first post-mortem had shown no sign of poison. Maybe the quinine and mercury in the medicines he had taken for his supposed malaria somehow concealed this or at least misled the analyst. It was further suggested that the reason why no arsenic had been detected might have been that those of Edmund's organs taken for analysis could have been confused with another set on the mortuary shelves.

As for Vera's high temperature, this had persuaded the doctors that she had succumbed to a particularly bad case of gastric flu. According to Sir Bernard Spilsbury who was in attendance at the inquests, it was also perfectly compatible with poisoning.

The Croydon police, led by the tireless Inspector Hedges, pursued these murders with great energy but by August the file was closed and whilst there were suspects, the case was never reopened. Even so, many people, not least the police, had their own views about who had committed the crime.

So round up the usual suspects. Round them up, these people from South Croydon and let us have a closer look at them. Can we gain the slightest hint of who was responsible for what has become one of the great murder cases of the 20th century?

Was there some random madman – or madwoman – who had set his sights on a particular family and had decided to wipe out three of its members? After all, the back door to Violet's house was often left open. And Grace's side door was frequently open during the day. Had a lunatic, loose in South Croydon, found an opportunity to spike Edmund's bottle of Bass? And after some months had he then gone into Violet's home, on at least one occasion to poison the soup and on another to doctor the Metatone? It is possible. But is it likely that this stranger, who might even conceivably be a family friend, would

The house where Vera and Violet Sidney died.

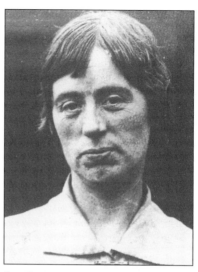

Kate Noakes, the cook.

manage to smuggle a bottle of Bass into the South Park Hill Road house and leave it in the larder? And later go to 29 Birdhurst Rise and seek out Mrs Noakes's soup, ready for the next day? And then another time to find the Metatone bottle? It could not be easy for a friend, less so for a total stranger.

Don't for a moment consider the cook, Kate Noakes. She had arrived on the scene only after Edmund's death. It was her misfortune to find herself in a house where there were two sudden deaths. Admittedly, she did not care for her new place and had expressed her intention to leave. Whilst she liked both Vera and Violet, she found the excessive meanness with food more than she could stand. She was rigorously investigated by Inspector Hedges and in the coroner's court and there could be no doubt about her innocence.

What about the possibility of Grace murdering her husband, her sister and her mother? Can it even be contemplated? Or what about Tom? Did he poison his mother, his sister and his brother in law? Or did Violet murder Edmund whom she so disliked and then for no discernible reason, her beloved Vera and then, horrified at what she had done, commit suicide? Are any of these likely candidates?

Look too at the means. There was arsenic available in each of the houses as weedkiller. Any member of the family had easy access to it just as each of them had similarly easy access to each other's homes.

50

Tom Sidney had it in powder form under the Eureka brand in his garden shed. A rusty tin of this powder had been found in Violet's garden but it was clear that this could not possibly have yielded the fatal dose. In the Duffs' cellar at the time of Edmund's death were two tins of Noble's weedkiller, one of them unsealed but corked. Possibly a small amount had been taken out of there. The Metatone bottle had contained a sediment, possibly of caustic soda, which was present in both of these preparations and which gave the nasty, gritty taste which Violet had noticed when she drank her tonic.

Could it have been Tom? Most certainly. Poor flurried Mrs Noakes could not be sure under cross examination but she thought she had seen him in the house on the day that Violet died. But Tom, a successful professional entertainer, was married to a wealthy American. He had none of the money troubles that beset the Duffs. Given that, it is also true that people do not murder solely for financial gain. Edmund was not terribly fond of his brother in law whose house he and his wife visited rarely. On the other hand Tom paid regular visits to the Duffs, to talk about his act and to try out new songs.

There is no doubt that Violet had fiercely disliked Edmund partly for his prodigal ways, partly because she thought him socially inferior even though he was well enough connected. But there was also another reason. Edmund had been introduced to Violet's daughter by her former husband, Thomas Sidney, the man who years earlier had deserted her and her children. By association, Edmund was hated by Violet who referred to him as 'that dreadful little man'. Had her constant disapproval encouraged one of her children – or both Tom and Grace, in the eyes of the coroner, though he was never able to reveal his opinion – to do away with Edmund?

But why after that does loyal, devoted Vera have to die? And why indeed does Violet? Is there madness here?

At one point during the inquests there were suggestions that more exhumations were possible and that the bodies of two of Grace's little girls, a seven year old dead since 1919 and a two year old dead since 1924, were to undergo post mortems. And there was the old lodger – yes, Grace had been reduced to letting a room to a paying guest – who had died in 1927 and whose death had been attributed to a brain haemorrhage. One witness had said that Miss Kelvey had been badly treated by Grace and that the old lady thought that Grace did not care for her husband, Edmund. She too was to be exhumed. But it came to nothing. They had three corpses already under discussion. Did they

Grace Duff.

really want six? And could they bear the thought of those two children ...?

Was it Grace then? Or Tom? Not both certainly. Not both acting in concert. Surely not. Grace, anonymous somewhere on the south coast where she lived until her death at the age of 87, gave no hint that she could supply any answers to this intriguing mystery. And Tom, in later years running a lucrative antiques business in America, made no announcements about his opinions.

In the 1960s Richard Whittington-Egan began his detailed researches into the mystery although he waited until Grace's death in 1973 before publishing *The Riddle of Birdhurst Rise*. He met several people who were involved in the case and reached very clear conclusions. Inspector Hedges was convinced that Grace had committed the murders. He had wanted to arrest her but his superiors felt that the evidence was just not strong enough. Her brother Tom had no doubt of her guilt. He said: 'I was advised by officers of Scotland Yard to put as much distance between myself and my sister as possible, for Grace was considered dangerous to my family. I did so and settled in America.' And Aunt Gwen Greenwell was sure of her guilt, while Dr Binning was of the view that she was a psychopath. To him she had always seemed too excited rather than shocked and saddened, as she stood at the death beds of her husband, her sister and her mother. Even Grace's brilliant counsel, William Arthur Fearnley-Whittingstall, came to the conclusion that he had been defending a triple murderess.

And the motive? Well, Edmund was, it appeared, a less than pleasant man, coarse, quarrelsome and crude in addition to being a spendthrift. She wished to be free of him. And it was suspected that she had been conducting an affair with Dr Elwell, then in his early fifties, and a noted philanderer. The other murders were apparently for the substantial sums that the deaths of Vera and Violet would bring her. Perhaps Vera suspected something, perhaps she disapproved of the relationship with the doctor, perhaps she threatened to stop paying John's school fees. And at the last, perhaps her own mother had had her suspicions.

But then, of course, Richard Whittington-Egan might have been misled. After all, these were for the most part only opinions. But whatever the case, these crimes were coolly committed, calculated, unbelievably cruel, always at the time when the victim was already off-colour or in Violet's case, at a low pitch. Not what one would have expected in such a respectable spot, among such upright people; not what you would ever consider in leafy South Croydon where the roads led away from the curtained claustrophobia of Birdhurst Rise to green Lloyd Park, to the woody heights of Croham Hurst, to Addington, Selsdon and then away into the fresher uplands of Surrey and Kent.

6

THE
CAMP FOLLOWER

The Murder of Joan Pearl Wolfe at Hankley Common,
September 1942

Somewhere near the top of the steep slope the attack began. Did he, angered beyond reason with his lover, pull out the knife and strike at her, aiming first at the head? Perhaps so for there were three shallow stab wounds in the front of her skull and her arms bore knife wounds where she had held them up to protect herself. Then, the blood pouring down her face, she had managed to stagger to her feet and run downhill for her very life. And her few possessions dropped from her handbag as she went. They were not to be found for some weeks.

He caught up with her down below, down in the thick woodland and scrub, three or four hundred yards away from where he had first attacked her. It was in that woodland, where the branches lacerated her face, where the undergrowth scratched her legs and tugged at her feet so that her shoes fell off, that he caught up with her after she fell over a military trip wire. She had fallen heavily onto her face and her two prominent front teeth, bearing the brunt, were knocked clean out. Perhaps it was that fall which fractured her cheek bone. Now, wretched and terrified, breathless and in pain, she lay face down. He crushed her skull with one blow of the birch wood stake. He concealed the body in the woodland under leaves and soil.

Later, a couple of days or so after she was killed, he came, most likely at night, and dragged her up the slope to the top again. How long can it have taken him, dragging her body by one arm, to reach the top? How long pulling her corpse across rasping soil which grazed the flesh, tugging it over tough little woodland growths which left ragged little scratches, releasing it momentarily when her dress snagged, when a limb lodged in some silent midnight place, refusing to move on? How long? An hour? With time needed to stop to catch his breath, to wipe his brow, to listen to the sounds of the night? When finally he reached the top he buried her in the shallowest of graves, under a light scattering of sandy soil no more than four inches deep.

Then several weeks later, on 7th October 1942, during a military exercise, tracked vehicles churned up the soil of Hankley Common. A hand reached up from its grave; a foot, too. And a soldier called the police. Superintendent Webb came from Godalming to look at the partly mummified body with its unrecognisable face. He must have assumed that this was some murder by a soldier. And if so his heart must have sunk for there were huge numbers of military hereabouts. British, Canadians, Americans, there were thousands of them, constantly on the move from one camp to another, from Thursley, from Witley and other nearby places. There were postings, secondments, temporary attachments, units on special exercises, an ever-changing population that could scarcely be kept track of. Webb must have considered the problem with some doubt of success and possibly Detective Superintendent Tom Roberts, Head of Surrey CID, who shortly joined him, might have been excused for being similarly pessimistic.

The following day Professor Keith Simpson, the Home Office pathologist and Dr Eric Gardner, the Surrey pathologist, arrived to advise on the exhumation. They found decomposition well advanced, the body heavily infested with maggots which had eaten much of the remains. The back of the skull had been shattered into several fragments by a violent blow.

Simpson and Gardner knew that this was not the first resting place of the body. The maggot infestation indicated that it had been either exposed to air or lightly interred for at least two days. This had allowed blowflies to settle and breed. Another indication was the scratching and tearing which had resulted from the body's being dragged from its original burial place. As for time of death, the pathologists estimated that it had occurred about a month earlier, basing their opinion on the fact that the heather under the body was not in flower. It had stopped flowering five or six weeks earlier.

The problem of finding a murderer in wartime Britain was difficult enough. So was the identification of dead strangers in a country in upheaval, in which there was a greater degree of movement of the civilian population than at any time in the country's history. The Surrey police, already stretched with the demands made upon it for security work, called in assistance from Scotland Yard. They sent the very experienced Detective Chief Inspector Ted Greeno and Detective Sergeant Fred Hodge.

There was no indication of who the murdered woman was. No one had reported her missing. She had been wearing a green floral summer dress, a slip and vest, a bra, French panties, and socks. Her shoes had been found near her body. Was she perhaps one of the numerous camp followers, girls who hung around military camps, offering their services in return for the glamour of uniform, for GI chewing gum and the dream of a home on the range, for promises of marriage to Yorkshiremen or chaps from Devon, for hopes of romance in Saskatchewan? There were many such girls locally, girls from all over the country, the despair of respectable Godalming.

Yet almost immediately there was a clue to her identity. PC Timothy Halloran from Godalming heard of the murder, saw the description of what she had been wearing and asked to see her clothes. Yes, he was able to say with confidence, referring to his note book, this was 19 year old Joan Pearl Wolfe. At 9.45 pm on 21st July the constable had met her in the street in Godalming. She was with two Canadian soldiers. She was a stranger to the town and clearly living rough and dressed like a tramp. But she spoke well; she wore a crucifix. To Halloran it did not seem right that a young girl should be in this condition. He was concerned that she had run away from home. She could be under age. He had insisted that she come to the police station with him while he checked her identity. He contacted her mother in Tunbridge Wells. Before she left the station Halloran asked that she come back the following day because he thought she was in need of help. Remarkably she did report to the police station the next day and was admitted to the Warren Road Hospital in Guildford, suffering from scabies.

The next time Halloran had seen the girl was on 21st August when he had gone in response to a call from the Canadian camp at Witley. They had reported her for being on the camp. He noted that she was wearing a distinctive dress with a green floral pattern given her when she was in hospital. Again she was filthy, louse-infested. The constable persuaded her to go to Warren Road again which she did. She discharged herself from the hospital on 1st September and never returned.

The third time Halloran saw her was in her mummified condition, but he could identify her for Greeno.

Auguste Sangret.

And oh yes, Halloran told Greeno, the first time that he had met her one of the Canadians from Witley had accompanied her to the station. The constable had recorded his name, too. He was Auguste Sangret aged 28 and serving with the Regina Rifles.

57

Poor Joan Pearl Wolfe, convent educated, regular Bible reader, escapee from a home where she had seen her father with his head in the gas oven, daughter of two step-fathers, seeker after love, anybody's love, any soldier's love, anybody who would promise to marry her. Yet what insights had she into her own neglected condition? Who would want to marry such a dirty creature, happy enough in her own sad squalor, able to settle in the deserted buildings, able to live in wigwams, the little bend-overs thatched with gorse and heather? Who would opt for a life-time of living like that with her? She had her lovers but they do seem to have been temporary adjuncts to her life. At least two, possibly several more, had promised marriage but ...

Over the weeks the skull – 38 separate pieces – was rebuilt. A birch pole which had been found, about three feet long and five inches thick, fitted the blow to the back of Joan's head. Stuck to it were eight hairs from her head. But the birch pole bore no fingerprints. It was the knife that had penetrated the girl's skull that the police needed, a knife with a curious point shaped, the pathologists said, like a parrot's beak.

Items that Joan had lost in her struggle and her desperate flight were, during the lengthy and meticulous search of the woods at Hankley Common, handed in. Crucifix, identity card, a sad little white elephant, a New Testament, a letter she had sent to Auguste Sangret telling him of her pregnancy, about their future marriage. 'You are all I have in the world,' she had written to him. At this time she had known the copper-skinned soldier for little over a week.

Private Auguste Sangret was an obvious person to interview and Chief Inspector Greeno asked the Canadian CO if he might interview the soldier. Sangret was asked to wait in the guardroom until the policeman arrived. Greeno then decided that he would interview the Canadian at Godalming police station and they motored there from Witley. On the way it is likely that conversation was informal and that Greeno learnt something of the man's background. He was half French, half Cree Indian and he had joined the army in 1940. He had never attended school and he was illiterate though intelligent. He had in fact been posted to Witley on a basic literacy course. Greeno was to describe him, betraying perhaps some of the attitudes of the period, as 'a handsome brute, stocky, not more than 5'7" tall ... shoulders tapering to a ballet dancer's waist. His hair was oily black and his face lean and swarthy.' Sangret had a reputation for being uncommunicative and sullen yet at the police station he willingly opened up to Greeno. He talked to the detective over a period of five days while Sergeant

Hodge took down 17,000 words in a statement 58 pages long. But five days? What about habeas corpus which ought to have released the man after 24 hours?

Sangret told Greeno how he had met the girl in a pub in Godalming in July. She was living rough. Her boy friend, her most recent prospective husband, had just been posted back to Canada but her sense of loss had not prevented her from making love to Sangret that night. From then until September they had met regularly and he had built her a series of wigwams in the woods. He had given her pies from the NAAFI, lemonade, small sums of money.

At one point Joan had squatted in a derelict cricket pavilion but she had been turfed out by an ARP warden and it was back to another wigwam. She left poems and prayers on the pavilion wall. And a poignant line: 'A. Sangret. Canada. J. Wolfe now Mrs Sangret. England September 9 1942.'

Sangret had been disciplined for spending nights with her off camp. He had spoken to his CO about marrying Joan but had made no formal application to do so. Then, on the day of his interview with Greeno, he had told the CO that he was no longer interested in her. She had gone away, he said. She hadn't turned up to meet him on 14th September as arranged. Sangret thought she might have gone off with another serviceman. Nevertheless, he had earlier reported her missing to the military police although not to the local police. But now he had another woman friend up in Glasgow.

It was after the statement was signed that Greeno showed Sangret his former girl friend's clothing. Until then the detective had kept all the information about the murder to himself although even if he was innocent the Canadian must have guessed something was amiss. After all, he had been interviewed for five days.

'I guess you found her. I guess I shall get the blame,' Sangret said when he saw the clothing.

'Yes, she is dead,' Greeno replied.

'She might have killed herself,' was Sangret's bizarre comment.

Nevertheless in his statement Sangret had said nothing to incriminate himself and there was no hard evidence to use against him. He was released without charge and went off on leave to Glasgow.

Greeno had no firm proof that Sangret had murdered Joan Pearl Wolfe although he was now convinced, from what the soldier had told him, that the murder had occurred on the night of 13th-14th September. As the interview had proceeded Greeno had Sangret's trousers and one of his blankets analysed for blood. On the blanket there were three suspicious stains. Had Joan, dying or already dead, lain on it? Were the stains her blood? But nothing conclusive came out of the analysis.

For the next several weeks the search for the knife continued. Where was Sangret's? He had been asked and replied that he had lent it to Joan so that she could cut bread and open tins. He claimed now to have no knife.

Not until 27th November, when the investigation was seven weeks old, was there a break-through. For some weeks the waste pipe in the wash house behind the camp guardhouse had been blocked and at last a soldier had been detailed to clear it. He had brought out the usual foul-smelling soggy mass of detritus but even that had not cleared the blockage. He had delved deeper and brought out a jack knife. Its tip looked as if it had been snapped off and refashioned into a shape resembling a parrot's beak. When it went to the pathologist's lab the tip of the knife was found to fit the wounds in the skull exactly.

Greeno now had the weapon. And now he had to find whoever had placed it in the waste pipe. He had no doubt that it had been put there on the morning when he had arranged to meet Sangret, when the soldier had been waiting in the guardroom for him to arrive. Greeno believed that Sangret had gone to the wash room and rid himself of the distinctive murder weapon.

Three soldiers identified the knife, a British army issue, as Sangret's. They recalled its curious tip. A military policeman remembered seeing it in August stuck in a tree near one of Joan's wigwams. He had handed it to the military police and a corporal MP identified it as the lost knife which he had handed back to Sangret.

When Sangret, now stationed at Aldershot, was brought back to be interviewed once more by Greeno, he admitted that Joan had lost a knife like the one he was now being shown but he denied that it had been returned to him by the military police. Certainly it had not been his knife, Sangret said. Joan had been given the knife by a former boy friend, he said, although this contradicted an earlier statement he had made.

Confident now that he had the murderer of Joan Pearl Wolfe, Greeno asked, as courtesy demanded, that Superintendent Webb of Surrey arrest the man. When he was charged the Canadian said: 'I didn't do it. Someone did but I'll have to take the rap.' Typical answer perhaps. Or perhaps, if he was innocent, just a philosophical acceptance that there was now no hope for him. And knowing his own poor record – petty civilian crimes and AWOL on several occasions – he might have feared the worst.

Certainly the hard evidence against Auguste Sangret was thin. No fingerprints on the birch pole; no blood on the knife. Whoever put the knife in the wash room was likely to have been the murderer. Did Sangret, summoned suddenly to the guardroom to wait for Greeno, rid himself of the tell-tale knife before his marathon interview? But no one saw him go to the wash room that morning.

Other witnesses were now found. Sangret had been talking about Joan's departure. He told one that he had sent her away because she was too scruffy; to another he said that she was in hospital; another heard that she had left him; to another he said that she might have killed herself. Yet if Sangret really did not know where she had gone he might easily have speculated about all of those possibilities.

There is strong circumstantial evidence which tells against the Canadian. There were soldiers who disliked the way in which he treated Joan. One told Joan three times to leave Sangret. Yet another said: 'I told Sangret to stop using her like a goddam squaw.' Not that any of this means that he killed her. And were there not several other soldiers in the area who knew Joan? Should he have been convicted solely on circumstantial evidence?

The opinion of Superintendent Tom Roberts was that Sangret tired of Joan who was pestering him to marry her. She was also claiming to be pregnant by him though this was never proved.

Perhaps Roberts was right but the proof always seems frail.

Auguste Sangret was found guilty of murder at Surrey Assizes in March 1943. He was sentenced to death and despite a strong recommendation for mercy he was hanged at Wandsworth the following month.

One question always remains – why was the body moved to the exposed top of the hill? Had it remained at the bottom of the slope where first buried perhaps it might never have been found. So why? Some say that it had something to do with the traditions of the Cree tribe, a ritual burial. Perhaps.

7

THE
BODY IN THE CHALK PIT

The Murder of John McMain Mudie in Kensington,
November 1946

The first time they met as a trio John
Ley did most of the talking. Oh yes, Ley told the others, he knew all
about blackmail and blackmailers. He'd had enough experience of
both. And so he had. Not only had he been a solicitor, but between
1922 and 1925 he had been Minister of Justice for New South Wales.
Later he had served in the Australian House of Representatives. No
need to tell him about blackmailers. He'd come across them often
enough.

Smith and Buckingham listened to the grossly fat man. Now a
wealthy property developer, Ley was worth listening to. Especially as
he had a job for them, the promise of some easy money.

The fact was that Ley knew two ladies who were being blackmailed.
They had come to him in desperation. They could, of course, go
through the due legal process and take the man to court. But that was
too slow, Ley told the men. Even then, it might backfire. In any event,
even if the ladies' names weren't published, those who knew them
would put two and two together. And no doubt put the worst
construction on matters. Their reputations would be ruined. And
anyway, this man, Jack Mudie, was a rogue. He had even seduced the
younger of the women.

But there was another way out. Stick and carrot, that was the answer.
Give the fellow a fright and then pay him off. Make sure that there was
enough stick and enough carrot to ensure that he didn't come back.

Money was not a problem. Ley would attend to that. But he was
going to need some muscle. This is where Lawrence Smith and John

The Reigate Manor Hotel as it looks today, now called the Reigate Hill Hotel.

Buckingham came in. Ley knew enough about Smith who was doing some building work for him at his Beaufort Gardens home in Kensington. Smith was the sort of man who would do anything for money. And the 6'4" former heavyweight wrestler Buckingham, now a taxi proprietor, had come recommended as a man who could look after himself and keep his own counsel.

But this blackmailer Jack Mudie had to be enticed up to London somehow. That was where they would deal with him. He had to be persuaded to come up to Beaufort Gardens from the Reigate Hill Hotel where he worked as a barman. After several meetings an elaborate strategy developed.

The plan involved the recruitment of two others. One was Buckingham's son, another John, built like his father. The other was Mrs Lilian Bruce, a housekeeper, the wife of a Putney bus driver and a friend of the Buckinghams. They were to inveigle Mudie to Beaufort Gardens where he would be 'cross examined', forced to confess to his crimes and then, after he had signed his confession, he would be given £500 and told to leave the country.

Several times in the autumn of 1946 an apparently very grand lady paid visits to the Reigate Hill Hotel. She was always attended by her chauffeur, a strapping young man in uniform. The lady was obviously much impressed by the hotel's Scots barman and they would talk very familiarly, sometimes about his service in the RAF from which he had been demobbed earlier in the year; sometimes about his failed marriage and how he was now settling well in a job he liked very much.

On one of her visits the lady told Mudie of a cocktail party she was arranging in London. Would he, she wondered, be interested in running the bar for her? She needed someone who was reliable, someone who knew his drinks. And Mudie, delighted, perhaps flattered, accepted.

On Thursday 28th November, Jack Mudie was picked up at the Reigate Hill Hotel and travelled to London with his hostess in her chauffeur-driven Wolseley. They arrived at the back door of 5 Beaufort Gardens in the early evening. It was already dark. The chauffeur opened the door and ushered Mudie into the passageway of the house. Suddenly the door behind him shut and the barman was locked inside. The lady and her chauffeur remained outside.

*   *   *

Walter Combes thought it was a bundle of rags. He couldn't be sure because the light was failing but he peered down again into the hollow. No, it was an overcoat. And a body.

Within an hour the police had arrived at the chalk pit, just off Slines Oak Road in Warlingham. They had a murder on their hands.

The body which was found that evening of Saturday, 30th November, lay in a shallow trench, recently dug at the foot of the slope. The overcoat was pulled up over the head. Round the neck was a rope, fastened in two loose half-hitches. There was a piece of green material round the throat which had evidently been used as a gag. Later, Dr Keith Simpson, the Home Office pathologist, and Dr Eric Gardner, the Surrey police pathologist, were to note that two ribs had been fractured after death. Otherwise, the injuries were not especially severe. The man, it seemed, had died of slow strangulation from the ligature round his neck, although exactly how was never completely resolved to Simpson's liking.

The dead man's shoes were clean. Obviously he had been killed elsewhere and carried over the slippery mud of the chalk pit to where he now lay. And whoever had done the carrying had been prepared to dispose of the body, for in the bushes, only yards from the corpse, was a pickaxe.

Murder victim, Jack Mudie.

And the identity of the dead man? A book entitled *One Hundred Cocktails* gave some kind of a clue. Letters in his pockets gave his name and workplace. Very soon, Detective Superintendent Tom Roberts and Detective Sergeant Frederick Shoobridge established that they had found Jack Mudie who had left the Reigate Hill Hotel two days earlier to go to a party in London. But they had no firm evidence yet that this was a murder case.

The national and local newspapers enjoyed this story of the body in the chalk pit. And they latched on to a further development in the tale. Two landscape gardeners, Frederick Smith and Clifford Tamplin, had been passing the chalk pit in the drizzling dusk on 27th November.

Their attention had been drawn to a small black car, an Austin or a Ford, in the chalk pit. This was unusual. Cars weren't often there at this time of day and in November, too. Then they had seen the man. And he had spotted them as well for he had run down the slope and into the car and had driven off in a hurry. Strange, they thought. And more than ever strange when they heard about the body. They hadn't got the registration entirely though they recalled the number – 101. And yes, they were sure of the day and the date. They had no doubt about that – 27th November, the day before Jack Mudie had left the Reigate Hill Hotel.

The Surrey investigators learnt that Mudie had received several calls from London in recent weeks. Phone calls at that time were recorded on paper at each exchange and then collated at Balham. Detective Sergeants Shoobridge and Cox went to Balham and cross-checked all London-Reigate Hill Hotel calls. It was a laborious task but it led them to a prefab on the edge of Regent's Park. It was the home of young Buckingham. Later in the day, when he learnt that the police had called, the young man contacted his father and Mrs Bruce and all three went to Scotland Yard where they were interviewed by Roberts. Here they described the stick and carrot plan and their participation in the events of 28th November. All the time they stressed that they thought they were punishing a blackmailer. More and more, they had learnt from the newspapers how decent and harmless Jack Mudie really was. And they had never thought that it would result in his murder. At this point Metropolitan Police detectives led by Chief Inspector Philpot became involved in the investigation.

On 17th December Lawrence Smith was arrested. The police had discovered that he had hired a black 8 hp Ford with the registration FGP 101. This tied up with the statement of the two landscape gardeners. Smith now gave an account to the police which was not significantly different from that which they had already heard from Mrs Bruce and the Buckinghams. He spoke of how Mrs Bruce and young Buckingham in his chauffeur's outfit had taken Mudie to Beaufort Gardens and how, once the barman was in the dark passageway, the door was locked from the outside. At once Smith had seized the bemused Mudie by the waist and the older Buckingham threw a blanket over his head. They bound him by the wrists and ankles and then forced him to hop along the passage to a room where they roped him in a swivel chair.

John Buckingham senior and Smith were in agreement up to this point. They disagreed about who gagged the murdered man. Buckingham claimed that he had left the house with Mudie still not gagged. Smith said that he brought a green French-polisher's rag from the kitchen and that he gave this to Buckingham to tie round the bound man's mouth.

Buckingham stated that he then met his son and Mrs Bruce in a pub and that he paid them £200 for their night's work. He told them that Smith had been asked by Ley to stay behind until some men who were going to extract the confession from Mudie turned up. For his part, Smith said that he left the house ten minutes after Buckingham when Ley's expected visitors came. He also said that on 2nd December he had met Ley, who told him that Mudie had signed his confession and had agreed to go to Australia.

On 28th December, when the police were satisfied that at last they had enough evidence, Ley, Smith and John Buckingham senior, were jointly charged with Mudie's murder. Later, when it became clear that Buckingham had not been present at the murder, he was discharged. He was to become an important prosecution witness.

Smith, however, was deeply implicated. Clifford Tamplin, the landscape gardener, identified him as the man who had driven off from the chalk pit on the 27th November, the day before Mudie's abduction. What could he have been doing there? Preparing a grave?

Furthermore, the pickaxe found in the chalk pit was identified as one which Smith had been using during his building work at 5 Beaufort Gardens.

At the Old Bailey trial of Ley and Smith in March 1947, a curious tale emerged. To begin with, Mudie was not a blackmailer. Secondly, he had never met Ley. The Scotsman had been murdered because of a stranger's ungovernable, obsessive jealousy. Ley believed that the 35 year old barman was having a love affair with Mrs Maggie Brook. And Mrs Brook, 66 years of age, had been Ley's mistress for many years.

Mudie had once spoken to Mrs Brook when they were both staying in Homefield Road in Wimbledon. She had moved in there temporarily while repairs were being done to her own house and it was a natural place to go, for her own daughter and son in law, the Barrons, were also renting a flat there. Only in passing, it seems, Mrs Brook, in conversation with Ley, had referred to Mudie. It was enough to create a seething fury, a rage for revenge in the outwardly sensible-seeming Ley. He would not have anyone taking liberties with Mrs Brook. After all, he had supported her financially for years, ever since she had been

John Ley, found guilty but ruled insane.

widowed and followed him from Australia to England; he had bought properties for her; he had made her a director of his firm, Connaught Properties; he met her every night, took her to dinner, to shows. She was his. How dared another man think of making her his lover? Hadn't Barron, her own son in law, and Romer, living in another of the flats, tried something similar? Hadn't they tried to conduct affairs with Mrs Brook? All three men in Homefield Road, Ley believed, had attempted to seduce her. Of course she had denied that they had tried anything but he knew. Two of them had got away with it but Mudie would not.

It is unlikely that Barron and Romer, two absolutely innocent men, both happily married, who had escaped Ley's insane rage even suspected what he might have done to them. But the total stranger, the equally innocent Jack Mudie, was not so fortunate.

Both Ley and Smith were found guilty of murder in what Lord Chief Justice Goddard described 'as remarkable a case as has ever been heard within the walls of this court.' Both men were sentenced to hang and their appeals against sentence were dismissed. Ley, known for his dubious business ethics as 'the Horatio Bottomley of Australia', was however certified insane and sent to Broadmoor where he died within months. Smith was reprieved and served a life sentence.

8

PATIENCE
IS A VIRTUE

The Murder of Margery Radford at Milford,
April 1949

When Dr Allison returned from his short break on the Saturday, he called in to his office at the Surrey County Sanatorium in the grounds of St Thomas' Hospital at Milford near Godalming. There is always something to catch up with after a holiday and perhaps Allison thought that he might as well face up to it. And after all, it was early evening and he knew he would not be interrupted. On the Monday it would be business as usual. Questions, decisions, interviews, letters, the whole rigmarole that went with being a Medical Superintendent. No, a couple of hours in the empty office and he would probably break the back of the stuff in his in-tray. Then on the Monday he would not have quite such a pile to wade through.

What he did appreciate was the fact somebody had apparently anticipated his return. Jolly thoughtful. Very nice of them to leave him a fruit pie and a few dessert plums. As he waded through the paperwork Dr Allison took a piece of pie. Within minutes, however, he felt queasy, not at all well. Later at home he was disinclined to eat dinner and was then violently sick. He had vomited and vomited and afterwards, looking at himself in the mirror, he saw that there were small haemorrhages on his face, and in his eyes some small blood vessels had burst. The pie, he decided, though you can never tell. After all, he had been away from home and it was easy enough to pick up something or other in strange places. For the rest of the weekend he was decidedly unwell.

On the Monday, 11th April 1949, Dr Allison returned to work, still not feeling one hundred per cent. He had a mild stomach ache and felt

70

generally out of sorts. In the course of the morning, his deputy, Dr Herington, handed him a letter. It was marked 'Confidential'. It had come with the pie, Herington explained, but in view of its confidentiality he had felt that it ought not to be left around the Superintendent's office over the week-end. Much wiser, he had thought, to hand it over to Dr Allison personally. So much for office protocol in the 1940s.

The letter contained quite devastating information. It was written by Mrs Lilian Formby, a close friend of a patient, Margery Radford, a 43 year old married woman from Sanderstead. Mrs Radford had had pulmonary tuberculosis from November 1942 and despite a period of remission from 1944 to early 1948, she was now very ill. She had been in hospital for several months and the doctors were not expecting her to survive the summer. But then, when Lilian Formby had visited her the previous week, Mrs Radford had confided her fears.

Margery Radford thought that her husband, Frederick, was trying to poison her. Although he did not visit her as regularly as he ought to do, considering that he lived and worked only a mile away in the laboratories of St Thomas' Hospital, he kept sending her parcels of food – cakes, pies, fruit, jellies, custard. And she had begun to realise that often after she had eaten the food he sent, she had been ill. On some occasions she had been so ill that she had lost the use of her limbs. This had gone on for some months.

The sick woman had become increasingly suspicious of her husband even though it was hard for her to accept that he could be so heartless. Surely, she had told herself in moments of doubt, he could not want her dead, couldn't be speeding up the inevitable for she herself knew she had not long to live. But now she had reached the point where she could no longer ignore the possibility that she was her husband's intended murder victim. After all, when she came to think of it, there had been occasions a year or two earlier when she had been unaccountably ill, once after eating ice cream and another time after drinking tea. At the time she had put it down to some mild stomach disorder, perhaps she had even suspected food poisoning. But she had never suspected poisoned food from her husband. Now he was going home to Sanderstead each week-end, endlessly preparing one after another tasty bite and having her father take them in to her. Fred could not be bothered to call in to see her and often long days went by without his paying her a visit.

And another thing, six weeks earlier when her father had visited her in hospital he had reported that one of her two sons had been sick for days after eating a jelly which Fred had prepared. That too had been intended for Margery. It all seemed to add up. And now, in the last ten days or so there were, first, the plums and then the pie. She'd been ill again after tasting them. Now Margery wanted help from Mrs Formby, her visitor. Would she take the pie and the plums to somebody who could do something?

Mrs Formby, unsure of what her friend had told her, had taken the pie and fruit home. She had wanted her husband's opinion. Tony Formby had listened to what his wife told him, perhaps a shade disbelieving when first he heard what Margery Radford had been saying about Fred. He knew that their marriage was rocky, was aware of the callous way in which Fred, living and working only minutes away from Margery's sick bed, so rarely visited her.

It is understandable that Tony Formby was sceptical at first. After all, in real life people rarely come across acquaintances who are trying to poison their wives. Was he to believe that a man whose wife was at death's door was hurrying the process along? It made no sense. Yet when he inspected the plums, when he saw a brown stain on the pastry, he felt that at least he ought to cover himself, telling his wife that perhaps this ought to go to the Superintendent. He would know what to do. He could arrange a proper laboratory analysis. And so plums and pie went to the hospital, made their way to Dr Allison's desk, and the letter went too, though unfortunately for the Superintendent this arrived rather late.

As soon as he read the letter Allison telephoned the police station at Godalming. This was an urgent matter, quite beyond his experience. Could a senior officer come over at once? Detective Inspector Crowhurst, at the sanatorium in double quick time, listened to the remarkable story, heard about Mrs Radford's fears and about the virulent effect the pie had had upon Allison on the previous Saturday evening. He straightaway agreed to send off the suspicious food to the Scotland Yard laboratories for analysis.

On the following day the police received the preliminary result of the analysis of the pie and the plums. Both contained arsenic in the form of potassium arsenite. They contained three times the minimum fatal dose for a healthy adult. With her frail body, Margery Radford required very little arsenic to take her off. And in fact, on 12th April, the very day that the result of the analysis was known, in mid-afternoon, the wretched woman died.

Others now mentioned to the police their uneasiness about Fred Radford and his relationship with his wife. A patient in a bed near Margery Radford's confided that for several weeks the poor woman had been prostrated whenever she had taken any of the food sent in by her husband. And Margery's father, James Kite, who visited her from Sanderstead every Sunday afternoon, confessed that both he and his daughter had been surprised at Fred's gifts of food, prepared by Fred's own hands. It was uncommonly unlike Fred to put himself out so. Possibly at the time they imagined that it was his way of making up for visiting so infrequently. And Mr Kite was to recollect that he himself had been ill when he ate some sausage meat that his son in law had prepared.

The police now asked the Coroner to order a post mortem and for this Dr Keith Simpson, the Home Office pathologist, was called in. His report on Margery Radford, who at her death weighed only 4 stone 13 lb, was completed on 13th April. Her death, he reported, was from chronic pulmonary TB and it had been hastened by arsenic. He had found a great quantity in the body – $6\frac{1}{2}$ grains. A mere two grains would have been enough. But the remarkable thing about this murder was that in any case Margery Radford was dying. No one had held out any hope for the poor woman. She was expected to die by the summer without any assistance from arsenic. All of her vomiting, all of her pain, her loss of movement in the limbs, had been attributed by hospital staff to the wasting illness from which she had suffered for years. Considering her tubercular condition, the poison can have accelerated her death by only a few weeks.

Margery Radford had been poisoned and her illness had been cleverly used to mask the fact. And she had been slowly and systematically poisoned. When strands of her hair were analysed arsenic was discovered at the roots and for a distance of 5 cm from the base. As hair grows at a rate of 0.44 mm each day, it was calculated that arsenic had been introduced into her food for the past three or four months.

So now to Frederick Gordon Radford, a man impatient for his wife's death but who at the same time used a slow and deliberate method. A medical laboratory technician, he knew what he was doing. And he was aware that whatever ill effects his poison demonstrated, the hospital staff would never suspect that his wife was being murdered.

On the morning of Friday, 15th April, Detective Inspector Crowhurst brought Radford into Detective Superintendent Tom Roberts' room at

HOSPITAL TRAGEDY OF HUSBAND

Found Dead on Day of Wife's Inquest

A few hours before an :-

POISONED FOOD SENT TO "WIFE" IN HOSPITAL

MURDER FOLLOWED BY SUICIDE OF "HUSBAND"

DOCTOR ILL AFTER EATING FRUIT TART

How a man murdered a woman, whom he bigamously married by poisoning her, and committed suicide a few hours before the inquest on her at Godalming on April 16th was told

before eating the tart, Dr. Allis: said the letter explaining the purpo. of the parcel was marked "Private and confidential," and his deputy had put it aside for him and witness did not see it until the Monday.

... ...auford's

It is understood the inquest

wife, atur- odal-)ora- lian evi- on rd, led ec- ter

Newspaper headlines at the time.

Godalming. The man certainly seemed anxious to clear matters up. He admitted to having a female friend, Ena Evans, and went so far as to admit that immediately after identifying his wife's body on the evening of 12th April, he had returned to his quarters in the hospital where Mrs Evans was waiting for him. There were also occasions during his day-long interrogation when he seemed evasive. At other times his recollection of events was uncertain. But he did admit to the purchase of pies and fruit. And why not? People in hospital like little gifts and there isn't much you can give them really. He had thought that pies and jellies and fruit would help with the inevitably monotonous hospital diet. But poison in them? No, no. Not him.

74

'I don't know anything about it. That means murder,' he told the police. 'I know it looks black against me. I admit I bought the pies and gave them to Mr Kite to take to my wife. Why should I want to kill my wife? I knew she was going to die anyway. I would not be such a fool as to use arsenic with my experience as I know the police would find it easily enough. If you think I did it, charge me and let a judge and jury decide.'

If Roberts and Crowhurst felt at the end of the long day's enquiry that they had identified Margery Radford's murderer, they were in no position to do much about it. There was not enough hard evidence. After all, others must have handled the food. What about Kite? Yes, Margery was his daughter but then she was Radford's wife. Or what about somebody in the hospital, some nurse or nursing orderly or even a doctor? Just because he was an unfeeling husband didn't mean that he was a murderer. Plenty of people could have tampered with the food.

The policemen ended their questioning at 10.30 pm and, considering the nature of their discussions, they and Radford appeared to part on reasonably good terms. In fact, Radford was motored back to St Thomas' by the police and he actually invited them in for a cup of tea. They felt obliged to refuse.

The inquest on Margery Radford was to take place the following afternoon at the police station and arrangements had been made for Radford to attend. He was not seen about on the Saturday morning and in consequence a porter was sent to his room. Fred Radford was found dead in bed. By his side was a suicide note. It read: 'I am tired of being badgered about something I know nothing about. The stuff that has been found in my wife's body is as much a mystery to me as to other people. I hope you will find an explanation for the whole thing. I also know that things look black against me but there you are. I have tried to do my duty but apparently have failed. All the best. F.G. Radford.'

The post mortem was conducted by Keith Simpson. Radford had taken prussic acid, one of the fastest acting poisons, in marked contrast to the arsenic which had contributed to his wife's death. He would have died within a couple of minutes, but long enough to dispose of the container which was never found.

Later when Radford's room was searched by the police, they found bottles of tablets and capsules including Nembutol, Amyl Barbitone and Soneryl, none of which could be obtained without prescription. They all came from his laboratory at St Thomas'. There had been endless opportunities for him to take home quantities of poison.

It was decided that the inquest on Frederick Radford should be held at the same time as his wife's. Consequently the hearing was postponed for a month.

It was now that more about Radford's background was revealed. He was an uncommonly handsome man, a ladies' man, who for the past two years had been having a passionate affair with Ena Evans. Living away from his Sanderstead home which he visited only at week-ends, Radford had considerable freedom to pursue this love affair. Early in January 1948, when Margery was still at home, Radford was telling his mistress that his wife was already in the sanatorium and that there was little hope for her. Was he already laying plans? He was even rashly suggesting that Ena could shortly move into the Sanderstead house with him. It seems evident that if Margery had not gone into the Surrey County Sanatorium, Fred Radford would have contrived some other way to poison her. After all, he knew his poisons. He was a qualified laboratory technician of great experience. But the need to make such plans evaporated when Margery suffered a relapse shortly afterwards and she was sent to the sanatorium.

Then, after the deaths of Margery and Fred, onto the scene came a woman who for the last 20 years had remained silent. The publicity of the case brought her forward. This was someone totally unexpected. It was Evelyn, his first wife. No, rather, it was Evelyn, his *only* wife whom he had married in 1926 and left in 1930. When he married Margery, Radford's marriage certificate described him as a bacteriologist – inaccurate; biochemist – inaccurate, and widower – particularly inaccurate. Evelyn had lost touch with her husband, knew nothing of his new life, knew nothing about his being a bigamist, had never sought him to maintain their daughter. Now he was in all the papers. She did in fact recall an occasion in 1928 when she was pregnant and feeling unwell. Fred had brought home something 'to buck her up'. But it had had a dreadful effect upon her. She took no more of the stuff. And now, over 20 years later, she could not but wonder.

On 19th May, the inquest jury, after deliberating for four hours, concluded that Frederick Radford had murdered his wife and had then committed suicide. The Coroner said that he believed that Margery never knew that she was not legally married. At least that was a small mercy. And it was further revealed at the inquest that Radford had three times in previous years, when he had flown into violent rages, attempted to poison himself.

What is surprising in all of this is Radford's impatience to kill off Margery. Why did he take such a risk? A few weeks more would have produced the longed-for result.

> Patience is a virtue
> Find it where you can
> Always in a woman
> Never in a man

It is a bit of a generalisation, that little verse. But in the case of Fred Radford, it is probably true. Why didn't he let nature take its course?

9

IF AT FIRST
YOU DON'T SUCCEED

The Murder of Frederick Gosling at Chertsey,
January 1951

Somebody in the Wheatash Cafe told
Fred Brown about the money. Old Fred Gosling had something like
£4,000, maybe more, hidden away in the house. You wouldn't believe
it, an old feller like him with all that money, and all from his little corner
grocery. The shop at Clay Corner, it must have been a gold mine and
Old Gossey, he'd been running it for 44 years. And you wouldn't think
he had two pennies to rub together. And Fred Brown, 27 years old, saw
prospects for himself in this. At the time, he was living with his sister
Phyllis and brother-in-law, Ernest Dodds, in Cranford Avenue in
Ashford. As he was to say later: 'If I had done it and got this money, I
should have been all set and been able to have got a place of my own.'

Anyway, somebody mentioned it to Fred and when on Wednesday,
10th January 1951, his elder brother Joe came round with a friend, Fred
talked to them about it.

Joe told Fred that he and his pal, Edward Smith, were going to go
into business together, selling logs from a lorry. And that was when
Fred told them about Old Gossey. There's an easier way of making
money, Fred said, easier than flogging logs. Perhaps the thought of
working from the lorry in that vicious, freezing winter of 1950-51, when
roads were iced up and snow-bound, was enough to convince Joe and
Edward Smith. And Smith was desperate for cash at that moment. His
fourth child was due in a fortnight and for the first time in his life, he
was out of work. A 33 year old lorry driver who has never before been
in trouble with the police must be desperate if he agrees so easily to
become involved in a robbery.

That night the three men took a bus from Ashford, calling in at The Holly Tree at Addlestone for a drink. Then later they went to Chertsey and walked down past the shop. Shouldn't be too difficult. It was a detached building. That helped. And the old chap, well, he was 79 and deaf. And he was on his own. He wouldn't put up much resistance. Smith and Joe Brown wanted to do the break-in there and then but Fred cautioned them. They hadn't a car. They'd need a car. Not tonight, they decided, but tomorrow. And so, the next evening, in a borrowed car, Joe Brown and Edward Smith turned up again at Ashford, ready for work.

At six o'clock the three men motored to Chertsey, parking the car in Wheatash Road. They walked round to Fred Gosling's shop. They had a plan worked out. They knew how the old man ran the place, that he had no cash register and that he always went for change into the room behind the shop. He had not moved with the times.

The men thought it would be easy. Smith and Joe Brown were to go into the shop to ask for a packet of 'Players'. They would tender a pound note. Then when the old man shambled into the back room for change they would follow him. Fred Brown, keeping watch outside by the phone kiosk, would at that point enter the shop, lock the street door, put up the 'Closed' notice and pull down the blind. Easy.

But things have a habit of going wrong. No sooner had the robbers followed Old Gossey into the back room and no sooner had Smith put his arm round his neck, than the shop door opened. Instead of Fred Brown, two schoolgirls came in. And Old Gossey, who contrary to expectation was struggling with his captor, let out a cry for help. At once the two men dashed out of the shop and into the street. They raced to their car just round the corner and drove off.

Then Fred Gosling, shaken, staggered into the street. He saw two men on the pavement edge. 'That's the man,' he shouted, pointing at one of them. But no. It could not be. Mr Dearden, a painter and decorator, explained that the man who he was talking to was not one of the robbers. He was a former workmate. And the two girls agreed. No, the man on the pavement had not been in the shop. In fact, Old Gossey had identified Fred Brown who looked so much like his brother Joe.

The police arrived and searched the area but found no one. They went away with a description of two scruffy men, both quite tall, who had attempted a robbery. They tried to reassure Gosling who was clearly alarmed. His face was slightly bruised but otherwise he was physically unharmed.

At about nine o'clock the next morning, 12th January, the milkman noticed that the side gate and back door to the shop were open. So was a larder window. But the shop itself was closed. He was used to seeing activity at the shop at this time. He entered the house calling out to the old man but there was no sign of him downstairs. But in the upstairs bedroom he found the body lying face down on the bed.

The old man's wrists had been tightly bound behind his back and then tied to the bedrail. His ankles too were tied and attached to the end of the bed. Old Gossey, eccentric in his personal habits, slept in his outdoor clothing and in that harsh winter he had kept on his jacket. This was pulled down from his shoulders, thus hindering his movement further. He had suffered a heavy blow over one eye. And he had been clumsily gagged with a thick white duster. He had died of suffocation. The gag and the restriction on his movement had contributed to his death.

The safe door in the bedroom was open and the key, taken from the old man's pocket, and a few coins, were scattered on the floor.

Downstairs in the room behind the shop, thousands of cigarettes and packets of tobacco lay in a dust sheet, as if ready to be carried off.

Gosling's corner shop (courtesy of Surrey Police records).

During their wait the men had thoroughly searched the sideboard and chest of drawers but in the end they had found no more than about £60. In the hearth there were 13 cigarette butts. Gosling's son was certain that they were not there when he called in to see his father after the attempted robbery. Had something obliged the robbers to spend enough time to smoke so many cigarettes in the downstairs of the house?

When Mr Dearden was questioned by Detective Superintendent Tom Roberts he mentioned that he had at the time of the robbery been talking to Fred Brown who had formerly worked with him. Fred had been standing by the telephone kiosk outside the shop and he had just gone over to him to have a chat. When Roberts spoke to Fred three days after the fatal robbery he was not convinced by his story that he was about to use the phone box. Fred told the detective that he was intending to ring a Mr Foster who lived in Staines about a couple of budgerigars that he had thought of buying. Yes, but why exactly was he in Chertsey? He did not have a very clear answer to that one. And no, Fred didn't think that he could give a very good description of the two men who had run out of the shop.

It was during a prolonged interview with Fred Brown that Roberts decided to ask Scotland Yard's criminal records office for further information about this witness. It transpired that one of his brothers, George, had escaped from prison and was still being sought. When had he last seen his brother, Fred was asked. Roberts was probably simply fishing. If so, the bait was taken. It had nothing to do with George, Fred told him. It was his other brother, Joe, they wanted.

Fred Brown explained how he, his brother and Edward Smith had weighed up the shop at Clay Corner on the Wednesday evening and how they had made an abortive attempt to rob it early on the Thursday evening. They had failed when Dearden came over to chat to him as this had stopped him from taking part in the robbery.

Later they had all met at Cranford Avenue. Fred had been sure that he had been spotted by the girls. He couldn't risk going back so soon. In any case, he believed that the police would be keeping a special watch on the house that night. But the other two, Smith and his brother Joe, were all for having another stab at it, Fred Brown told the superintendent.

According to Fred, on the Friday morning at about eight o'clock, Joe and Edward Smith came back to see him. They had done the job, they said, and had left Old Gossey tied up on the bed. He was quiet when they came out, they told Fred. Apparently, they had got in through the larder window and found nothing downstairs. Presumably because he was so deaf, Gosling did not hear his intruders rummaging around. When they went upstairs, however, he woke up and started to shout. They had tied him up.

Fred Brown's interview with Superintendent Roberts lasted the greater part of a day. Eventually, he made a deal with the detective. In return for immunity, he agreed to act as prosecution witness in any case relating to the Clay Corner crime that might be brought against his brother and Edward Smith. As yet, the charge was only assault with intent to rob. But in time, when there was enough evidence, Fred Brown knew that there would be a murder charge to answer.

Following Fred Brown's interview with Superintendent Roberts, Joe Brown was placed under arrest. Questioned by Chief Inspector Sidney Tappenden he claimed to have been in bed at his home in Peckham on the night of the murder. And at six o'clock on the evening when the failed robbery took place? He had been in London, he said. Confident that he had found the guilty man – guilty at least of the first robbery if not yet of murder – Tappenden cautioned Joe Brown, charging him with assault with intent to rob Frederick Gosling. As yet Tappenden and Roberts did not feel that their case for a charge of murder was strong enough but there was the forensic evidence from the cigarette butts which they hoped might be helpful.

Edward Smith was similarly charged. He claimed to have been at home painting on the evening and night of Thursday, 11th January. Yes, he said, he had been with the Brown brothers on the Wednesday night and, yes, they had had a long walk which might have taken them past Clay Corner, but he had not been there on the Thursday. 'If God knows I am innocent, he will protect me,' he said. 'I didn't come back again on the Thursday.' But later, after Dearden had identified him as one of the men who ran out of the shop, Smith admitted that he had taken part in the first failed attempt but not in the robbery that led to the death of the old man.

On 15th January all three men appeared before the magistrates on an assault charge. This was then changed to a charge of murder. At this point Fred Brown was discharged.

In police custody Smith constantly spoke of his predicament, the fact that this was his first offence, that his wife was expecting their fourth baby, that he had been horrified to see a newspaper heading on the day after the break-in: 'The Murder at Cosy Corner.' Was it a murder? he would ask. 'If you tie something round somebody's mouth, they can still breathe through their nose. They can breathe through their nose for ever, come to that.' He was distressed at the death of Frederick Gosling. Later Phyllis Dodds, the sister of the Brown brothers, told the court how Smith had wept on hearing that the old man had died.

At their trial at Kingston in March 1951, the star prosecution witness was Fred Brown. He admitted formulating the original plan to rob the shop at Clay Corner but, he said, after the miserable failure early in the evening he had refused to try a second time.

It was a remarkable trial where one man bore testimony against his brother. And Phyllis Dodds also appeared in the witness box. Yes, she had heard the men discuss the failed robbery that night. All three had been in the house at Ashford and had talked matters over. Asked about her part in the discussion she said: 'I think that it was very foolish. I did not say anything to them. They are men, not babies, old enough to know right and wrong. I had trouble of my own, my son in hospital.'

Phyllis Dodds told the court that Fred had not gone out again that night but that Joe and Edward had gone off to complete the task. Not only that, they had come back next day and reported what had happened though they had not said that Gosling was dead when they left the house. She also explained the reason for the 13 cigarette butts left in the downstairs room. When they had broken into the safe and taken the money, the two men had come downstairs and prepared to make off with thousands of cigarettes. They had carried these to the car which they then found had a flat battery. Fearing they might meet the police at that time of morning – it was probably about one o'clock – they returned to the house and stayed there until five or six o'clock. They then left, locking the money in the car, and walked back to Ashford. After that, Joe had taken the battery out of the lorry and a neighbour had given him a lift back to the abandoned car which, fitted with the battery, he then drove back to Cranford Avenue.

Ernest Dodds was equally adamant that Fred had not gone out late on the night of the murder. After the failed attempt, when the three men were discussing what they should do, Dodds told the court that Fred had said to the others: 'Don't go back. It's a bad omen.'

The forensic evidence which told most powerfully against Joe Brown and Smith came from the cigarette butts found in the downstairs room. The butts had been tested at the Metropolitan Police laboratory. Saliva samples indicated that six had been smoked by a Group A secretor and six by a Group B secretor. One cigarette butt was negative. Joe Brown fell into Group A and Edward Smith in Group B. If those cigarettes were smoked by the intruders that night – and there was strong evidence to show that there were no cigarette ends in the room when Gosling's son visited him in the course of the evening – then there was powerful circumstantial evidence pointing in the direction of Joe Brown and Edward Smith. Fred Brown, a Group O secretor, was cleared as far as the cigarette evidence was concerned.

The car that had been used for the robbery was traced. Not only was it identified by the neighbour who had given Joe Brown a lift back to Chertsey with the battery, but forensic examination revealed goat hairs in the car. These were proved to have come from three goatskin rugs in the old man's bedroom. Smith admitted that he had recently burnt an overcoat although he denied that he had done so because it was covered with goat hairs.

The defence argued that Fred Brown and another person had gone back to the shop late at night and that they were responsible for the death of Old Gossey. A prisoner in Bristol gaol said that while on remand Fred had admitted this to him. And leading for the defence, Derek Curtis-Bennett highlighted the unusual nature of a murder case where one brother testified against another. 'Are you therefore going to say this case is proved beyond all reasonable doubt,' he asked, 'when the substance and weight of this case depends on the evidence of Frederick Brown who, in my submission, has lied in order to get himself out of the dock, and similarly the evidence of his sister and brother-in-law?'

To no avail. Joe Brown and Edward Smith were found guilty of murder and executed on 25th April 1951.

But can Fred Brown's testimony be believed? Probably yes. Was he out to save his own skin? Again, probably yes. But how was the old man killed? Might it have been sheer incompetence, a faulty gag, that ended his life? Was it in fact a murder or was it manslaughter? They do at this distance in time seem to be more important questions.

As does the final question. Is blood really thicker than water?

10

THE
RAILWAY MAN

The Murder of Maartje Tamboezer at East Horsley,
April 1986

He got her, the cyclist, in the narrow lane alongside the railway track. When she had seen the length of nylon wire neck-high across the path she had dismounted. And that is when he got her.

He'd forced her into a field and then into a nearby wood. There were bluebells there. It was mid-April. Springtime.

When she was found, she had been bludgeoned, raped and strangled. She was 15. She was Maartje Tamboezer, a Dutch girl, who had been living in England with her parents for some years. She had been on her way to buy sweets.

He'd left traces, of course. There was a length of nylon, manufactured in West Germany, and used extensively by British Rail. There was some yarn of Swedish manufacture. There were some used Swan Vestas that he had used to set fire to the tissues that he had pushed in her vagina. There was a sock shoved down her throat. Her thumbs and wrists were tied behind her back. He had strangled her, using a piece of wood twisted into her belt as a tourniquet.

This was his second murder. The signs were there. It was him.

A witness described a small man going for the 6.07 from East Horsley. But none of the two million railway tickets checked for fingerprints ever yielded anything.

In the wake of the horrific East Horsley murder, committed on 17th April 1986, Surrey CID set up Operation Bluebell, its name commemorating the woodland spot where the murdered child had been found. This investigation was headed by Detective Superintendent John Hurst. At the same time an investigation was being conducted into another, earlier murder. Detective Superintendent Charlie Farquar of the Metropolitan Police was investigating the killing of a 19 year old secretary, Alison Day, on 29th December in the previous year. Alison had been on her way by train to meet her boy friend at Hackney Wick. Her murderer had forced her off the train and taken her to a rat-infested garage block in Hackney. Here he had tied her hands behind her back and raped her before hitting her on the head with a brick. Then he tore her shirt and used it to garrot her with a tourniquet, known to carpenters as a 'Spanish windlass'. He carried the body to the river and after weighting her sheepskin jacket with stones, threw her into the water. Divers found her 17 days later. The only forensic evidence was some clothing fibres, which were later to be used as conclusive evidence against her murderer.

Months later, Superintendent Farquar, looking at the BBC programme *Crimewatch* featuring the murder of Maartje Tamboezer, was struck by the similarities to Alison Day's murder. He contacted the Surrey police to compare the details. Together, the police of both forces recognised unique factors. Never before in a British murder had there been an attempt to set fire to a body in the pubic region. And there were other features – the tourniquet, the tying of the hands behind the back, the gag, the cutting of clothing for the ligature. In April 1986, the police were confident that one man was responsible for both murders.

There was another major investigation team at this time. This was Operation HART led by Detective Superintendent Ian Harley. From 1982 police in London and the Home Counties had been investigating a series of increasingly violent rapes. Initially, these had been carried out by two men, usually wearing balaclavas and dressed as joggers. They carried knives. By 1985, however, the police were certain that only one of the men was still active and responsible for perhaps as many as 30 offences. And he was increasingly dangerous. In one night in July 1985 he had raped three women.

Here too were some features common to all the rapes and to the two murders. For example, the rapist tied the hands of his victims, often with their own tights; after the attack, to conceal possible evidence, he burnt the paper tissues with which he wiped down their private parts. Then he would take a further precaution, combing the pubic hair of any further traces. And curiously he sometimes engaged his victims in conversation, sometimes seeming to be concerned and helpful. The proximity of a railway station was another recurrent feature. Did this man have some railway connection? Was he a railway buff, a train spotter, a railway worker?

His manner of approach was also identifiable. Sometimes, he would speak briefly to his intended victim and then after she had gone by, he would turn and grab her from behind. But the descriptions given to the police were not always helpful. Though the man was sometimes without a mask, he was described by his victims variously as having short black hair or longer ginger hair. His height was estimated as between 5'6" and 6'0". Many times and more accurately, victims referred to his staring eyes.

From police records throughout the country, HART (Harley's Anti-Rape Team) had gathered the names of all possible suspects. Every man in the country involved with violence towards women was on the computer list. But there seemed to be no logic to where the rapist might strike next. He had the whole of London and areas beyond the bounds of the metropolis in which to commit his offences. Among other places reports of his activities came from Hampstead and Barnes Common, Brent Cross and Kentish Town, Richmond and Hadley Common. They were miles apart, most frequently near railway stations. He knew the railway system and could turn up anywhere in the Greater London area and beyond, up into Hertfordshire and south into Surrey. By the autumn of 1986 every railway station along the North London Link from Docklands to Richmond was under police surveillance.

The number of suspects was gradually reduced as detectives considered individual cases: the dates made it impossible for some to have committed the offences; others had died; yet others were out of the country. But it was slow. By August 1985, there were still many suspects on the list and others being added. At that time the police did not know that the serial rapist they were seeking had just been added to the suspect list. This was John Duffy, who had no previous record of sexual offences.

Duffy, now in his late twenties and described variously as weak, polite, quiet, lazy, immature and insignificant, was a small man – 5'4" – very conscious of his lack of height. He threw himself into martial arts with great enthusiasm believing that this could compensate for what he regarded as personal inadequacies. Duffy was capable of extreme violence and frequently attacked his wife whom he blamed for their not having children. It was, in fact, Duffy's low sperm count which was the cause of their childlessness. His wife left him when she could no longer

The Surrey police force took part in Operation Trinity to try and track down the killer (courtesy of the *Surrey Advertiser*).

bear his viciousness and his excessive and frightening sexual demands. The nice man she had married had taken to tying her up before sex. She feared that he was going to kill her.

Even after she left him, Duffy called on his wife and forced her to have sex with him. He had turned, she said, into 'a raving madman with scary, scary eyes.' Terrified of him, she was to tell the court: 'You could not stare at him. You had to look away ... You would remember his eyes.' If they recalled nothing else, many of the women he attacked remembered Duffy's staring eyes. In July 1985, Duffy broke into the house where his estranged wife was living. He attacked both her and her boy friend. Both victims ended up in hospital after enduring a rain of karate blows. Duffy had also threatened the man with a knife.

Nevertheless, even though he was now placed on the HART list, Duffy was not considered a serious candidate for the title 'the railway rapist'. His offence, serious though it was, did not quite fit the pattern of the hooded man being sought by Operation Hart. All the same, despite the low priority they gave him, the police did oppose Duffy's being bailed at Acton Crown Court in August. They were unsuccessful in this. During the time of his worst excesses, when he committed his three murders, John Duffy was out on bail.

In September 1985, a 20 year old woman was raped in Copthall Park, near Barnet. After much sifting and rejecting of possible offenders, detectives assigned to the case considered that Duffy might be responsible for the attack. The girl had described a man with staring eyes, ginger hair and acne and this fitted Duffy. But on 2nd December the girl, still traumatised by her frightening experience, still obliterating her ordeal from her mind, failed to pick Duffy out at an identity parade.

For Duffy this was a close call. What if she had recognised him? It was a significant moment in the career of 'the railway rapist'. He decided in future to leave no witnesses. On 29th December 1985, he met Alison Day.

On 12th May 1986, less than a month after the murder of Maartje Tamboezer, Duffy was picked up by police a long way from his Kilburn home, loitering near the quiet Essex railway station at North Weald, not far from Epping Forest. He had been recognised as a man on bail for assaulting his wife. He was searched and found to be carrying a silver butterfly knife. To explain his weapon Duffy said that he was a Zen Budo martial arts enthusiast. The knife was confiscated, the police hoping that his former wife could identify it as the weapon used in his attack on her and her boy friend. They did not charge Duffy with possessing an offensive weapon. At that point Duffy had not been interviewed by the rape and murder enquiry team and there is doubt whether the team ever received information about this highly suspicious occasion.

But Duffy was undeterred by meeting the police at North Weald. The urges which drove him were ungovernable. Six days later on Sunday, 18th May 1986, a mere 31 days after the East Horsley murder, 29 year old Anne Lock, a recently married woman, on her way home from the London Weekend Television studios where she worked as a secretary, disappeared. She had arrived at Brookman's Park station in Hertford-shire at 10 pm. The search team found the cycle she had left at the station. But all other trace of her was lost.

Nine weeks later, Anne Lock's badly decomposed body was found among the brambles by the railway line. There was a ligature. Her hands had been bound behind her back. One sock had been shoved in her mouth and another had been used to blindfold her. An attempt had been made to burn the body. Although there was little forensic evidence after so long an exposure in the open air, the obscene murder bore the familiar signature of the killer of Alison Day and Maartje Tamboezer. It was assumed that she had been met on the train or just after getting off it, that her killer had forced her at knife point down the path from the station and had then urged her in the dark along the overgrown railway embankment.

The police had now set up Operation Trinity, a massive combined investigation under the overall direction of Chief Superintendent Vincent McFadden of Surrey CID. He was responsible for coordinating the enquiries of the four police forces involved – Surrey, Hertfordshire, the Met and the British Transport police. HART, now under Superintendent Ken Worker, John Hurst's Operation Bluebell and Charlie Farquar's team were in this joint operation. It was the biggest manhunt since the search for the Yorkshire Ripper. Five thousand suspects, sifted by age, method of attack, links to railways and other factors, had been reduced to 1,999.

On 17th July, some days before the discovery of Anne Lock's body, Duffy was interviewed by the police. He was among the 1,999 'Z men', those suspects whose blood tests matched samples from Maartje Tamboezer or whose blood group was unknown. Although there seemed to be nothing on which to hold him, it must have seemed odd that Duffy came to the interview with his solicitor and perhaps even more odd that he refused to give a blood sample.

The following day Duffy presented himself to West Hampstead police station, claiming to have been violently mugged in the street. He had a chest wound which was bleeding heavily from a razor cut. He had also been hit on the head and said that he was suffering from a complete memory loss. That day he was admitted to Friern Barnet Mental Hospital as a patient.

But there had been no mugging. Twenty year old Ross Mockeridge, like Duffy a martial arts enthusiast, had been persuaded to help his friend to fake the story. 'John handed me the razor,' Mockeridge was to admit at the trial. 'As he was talking, I got him with the razor so it was not painful as much as if he was bracing himself for it. It was a slashing movement on his chest. I was very shocked and said, "Oh, God, what have I done?"' And Mockeridge would also say: 'He asked me if I had considered rape and said it was a natural thing for a man to think about.' Duffy paid £100 for Mockeridge's service, all part of a plan to remove himself from police scrutiny.

Certainly, the net was closing on Duffy. Superintendent Hurst of the Surrey CID, working as a member of Operation Trinity, had had a squad of a dozen detectives focusing on the case. But he needed a more specific pointer and that was to come out of the work of David Canter, Professor of Applied Psychology at the University of Surrey.

Some years earlier Professor Canter had worked with the Bradford constabulary after the fatal fire at the football stadium, but never before had he been involved in an analysis of crime. Now, for the first time, he was working at the university with seconded police officers: Detective Constable Lesley Cross and Detective Constable Rupert Heritage of the Surrey CID, and Detective Inspector Jim Blann of the Metropolitan Police. They looked at maps, talked to witnesses, discussed matters with other officers, considered statements, analysed thoroughly scenes of crime. They placed their findings on computer. One day, it would help them unlock the mystery of the man they sought and would produce a psychological profile which would lead to his capture. All the time they were looking for hints. They wanted answers to certain questions. Who was their quarry? Where did he live? How did he operate? What did he say, what did he do to the women he raped? What was his background? And they felt that somehow the man's behavioural patterns would reveal the answers to their questions. Who was this rapist who on occasion had been considerate to the women he had violated? Who was he, this man who at times offered a cigarette, money for the train journey home, information about which train to take? Why had he gone on to become a murderer?

In September 1986 David Canter produced the Psychological Offender Profile describing a man who lived in the Kilburn-Cricklewood area of north-west London. This is where the rapist had begun his offences back in 1982. The rapist, Canter and his team reasoned, would have begun in a district he knew. And it was through a concentration on the most banal items that the profile was built up. Their man was married though his marriage appeared to be going through a turbulent period. In fact, Duffy was now divorced and his former wife had taken out an injunction to prevent him from seeing her. He was a loner, a man with one or two close male friends. He was a semi-skilled worker in a job which brought him into little contact with the general public. The profile was to turn out to be correct in 13 out of its 17 major indicators. 'A criminal leaves evidence of his personality through his actions in relation to a crime,' Canter wrote. 'Any person's behaviour exhibits characteristics unique to that person.' He was unable to say who the man was but he and his little team were able to suggest that some of these characteristics were to be found in the man they knew as 'the railway rapist', the man who had become a murderer. Canter's profile finally confirmed that Duffy was the man on whom the detectives must concentrate.

A picture of John Duffy at the time of his arrest
(courtesy of News International Syndication)

All of the invisible clues of behaviour pointed to John Duffy. Only he in the long list of suspects fitted the profile so well. Only he lived in Kilburn. But he was in Friern Barnet being treated for amnesia. As yet there was no hard evidence against the man.

Then on 21st October 1986 a 14 year old schoolgirl was held up at knife point near Watford Junction station. The man had come up to her quite casually. He had asked her the time and then grabbed her and forced her into woodland. She was gagged, blindfolded and with her hands tied behind her back, she was raped against a tree. On this occasion, the rapist's mask slipped but he let her go.

Duffy? But Duffy was at Friern Barnet. How could it be him? Patients did not just walk out of places like that. They were under strict supervision. Then the detectives discovered that he was not an in-patient. He had freedom to roam.

From now Duffy was followed wherever he went by Hurst's surveillance team. One night they decided to pick him up on the way to Copthall Park where a year earlier he had raped a woman. He was equipped with his balaclava, his string and his knife, his Swan Vestas and his tissues, the complete John Duffy murder kit.

A search of his home and that of his mother produced further forensic evidence which was used in court. In his mother's house the special yarn that he used to bind his victims was found. Fibres on

Alison Day's body matched one of Duffy's sweaters.

In February 1988, John Duffy, the former British Rail carpenter who had been sacked for bad time-keeping, still claimed a complete memory blackout. Described at his trial as 'very intelligent, cold and calculating', Duffy was sentenced to 30 years for the murders of Alison Day and Maartje Tamboezer. There was insufficient proof that he had murdered Anne Lock but the police closed the file on that crime. In addition he was found guilty of five rapes between June 1984 and October 1986 although the police put the figure at nearer 30.

Eleven years later, in March 1999, at the Old Bailey, Duffy pleaded guilty to nine rapes, six conspiracies to rape and two burglaries. He admitted to the rape of Anne Lock but as he had already been before the court and found not guilty of her rape and murder he could not be charged again. He admitted that his first rapes were committed when he was 17.

The search for John Duffy, that cunning predator, took a considerable time. It was extremely complex and despite the criticisms sometimes levelled at the investigators it has to be accepted that not until late did 'the railway rapist' appear on any list of suspects. And even when he did, he was buried deep down, a not very likely candidate. For years the police knew so little about the man they sought. He lived in the London area. But who was he among the millions living there? Who was the hooded rapist who might strike anywhere? It had been a daunting task.

11

MURDER
OFF THE M25

The Murder of Peter Hurburgh at Fickleshole,
December 1988

Call it the biggest car park in the
world if you want but the M25 has been a boon to many travellers.
Think of all those car trips from south to north if you had to go through
London. And what about east to west? What about getting snarled up if
you went that way? Or using the old circular route? Do you remember
competing with trucks and lorries when you went that way in the old
days? No, the M25 has been a blessing.

It's ideal for anyone wishing to go just a few miles. You can drop in
at one junction and provided that the road isn't too congested, make a
very quick trip of several miles and then cut off at another junction. And
at night when there's not too much traffic about you can really lap up
the miles. It's a godsend, the M25.

The trouble is that it is also a godsend to people who use it for the
wrong purposes. And it's ideal for criminals needing to make fast
journeys. And the criminal gang who for a few brief weeks in 1988
terrified householders on the south side of the M25 found it a
marvellous help. And make no mistake, during its short career this gang
was terrifying. Fortunately, their progress was halted firmly and quickly
but not before they had introduced nightmare to the Surrey stockbroker
belt. Small wonder that the police issued special warnings about the
gang, advising householders to take extra care and to ensure that their
doors and windows were securely locked at night. From early
November until mid-December 1988, as wicked, violent and cruel a
gang as has ever disfigured the county made a frightening if short-lived
appearance.

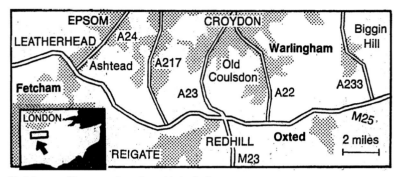

Sketch map of the area where the raids took place.

The three or four members of this gang, which used the orbital motorway to make getaways as well as to travel to other destinations, were always masked when they descended on their unsuspecting prey. They carried knives, a machete and a handgun and these they used in a series of aggravated burglaries. And after one robbery they were to be given the name, 'the kill for kicks' gang. But this was after their final jaunt. The escalation in violence was particularly alarming and had they not been caught it is not unlikely that there would have been other deaths. Certainly, other innocent people would have been treated to the gratuitous violence which characterised their raids.

The M25 gang first imposed themselves on the police mind in the autumn of 1988. From then they were aware of three young men – two white men and a black man, they thought – who entered houses and with threats of extreme violence and sometimes with actual physical brutality, stole what took their fancies and then made off with the car.

The activity as well as the violence hotted up on 6th November with a raid in Smitham Downs Road in Coulsdon. The following day, the gang made off with a Peugeot from a house near Morden. On 2nd December, gang members, armed with a knife and a handgun, entered a newsagent's shop in Byward Road, Shirley, terrifying the paper boy and stealing from the proprietor £200 and some jewellery. Two days later a house in Woodlands Road, Ashtead, was burgled.

At 3.15 am, on 5th December, a house was entered at Old Coulsdon. Again the frightened householders were menaced with a gun and knives. But this time, the gang's threats were realised. The wife and husband were blindfolded and tied up. The husband was locked in a bathroom whilst his wife, her baby only feet away, was raped on the bed. The gang took off in the family's Toyota. On the same day the

95

Peugeot stolen at Morden a month before was recovered. It contained some of the items stolen from Ashtead a few days earlier.

After a burglary in Bromley on 8th December, when a Citroen was taken, the stolen Toyota was found abandoned. The gang then returned on 9th December to another house in Woodlands Road in Ashtead. Here James Johnstone and his wife were threatened and tied up. The Citroen was left here and the Johnstone's blue Volvo hatchback was stolen. The next day, alerted to the theft of the Volvo, a police patrol car chased the vehicle for several minutes but in the heavy morning rush hour traffic in Gypsy Hill they crashed into another car and were obliged to abandon the chase. The car was later found abandoned at Gatwick airport. The two occupants of the car, the police said, were black men.

Some kind of pattern was emerging. The gang used threats and physical violence on victims who were often in no position to retaliate. Even when their victims were bound up, the gang members appeared to delight in continuing with their menacing behaviour. Furthermore, they seemed to be random in their choice of victim. Sometimes, the houses they entered were substantial and it was obvious that there were rich pickings to be had. But others were more modest and the risks that they took and the level of menace that they employed were out of all proportion to their gain. For example, the last three burglaries netted them about £4,000, not a great amount when the possibility of a stiff gaol sentence was weighed against the money. As for the cars, there was apparently no market for these. Or if there was, this gang had no access to it for most of the cars they stole were recovered.

So why did these men involve themselves in these risky, dangerous enterprises? Admittedly, criminals often come away with not especially rich hauls but very rarely do they engage in such a campaign of terror. Was it theft that really mattered to these men? Or was it something different? Was it the exercise of power which drove them? Was it the thrill of seeing their victims afraid, as undoubtedly they were? Who would not be intimidated when confronted by three or four snarling, shouting, hooded men? What hapless householder would feel sure of himself under his own roof when faced by such a fearsome gang? Who would not fear for his wife and baby? Who would not be cowed at the sight of a husband or son threatened by knife or machete or gun?

But it was on the night of 15th December that the M25 gang perpetrated its worst offences. It is as if everything had been building up to this. That night at about 11.30, a 57 year old hairdresser, Peter

Hurburgh and one of his former employees, 20 year old Alan Eley, were sitting in Hurburgh's Austin Healey car which was parked in a field. They had been for a drink at the White Bear, Fickleshole, and were on the point of leaving when they saw a shadow at the car window. Three men ordered them out of the car at gunpoint. They were told to hand over what money they had. But Peter Hurburgh resisted. He would not be treated in this way, he told them. Nor would he be silent. Who were they to tell him what to do? He struggled as they bound him with electric flex and then gagged him. Still struggling, Hurburgh was pushed to the ground and as he lay there, unable to protect himself, he was repeatedly kicked.

While his companion lay on the ground, Eley tried to make a break and run for it but he was caught and dragged back to where Hurburgh still wrestled with his bonds. The gang started beating the older man again, stamping on him, kicking him, and now he began to fight for breath, his eyes staring in panic. 'Doesn't he make a good actor?' one of the men laughed. Perhaps they did not know of his heart condition. But then, would these men have cared? It was now that they produced the petrol can and began dousing their two helpless prisoners. Young Eley passed out when he saw the lit cigarette being waved over his petrol-doused clothing. When he came to, the three attackers had gone. He struggled free of his bonds and went to the prostrate body of Peter Hurburgh, trussed up like a chicken. He was dead.

The post mortem was to show that Peter Hurburgh, a man with a serious heart condition, had been beaten so badly that he died of heart failure and shock. His body had blister burns consistent with unburnt petrol, head and chest injuries and superficial cuts to his ears, arms and thumb. He had five broken ribs and his fractured breast bone had been driven inwards almost touching the heart. In the opinion of the pathologist his injuries were consistent with his having been stamped upon.

The gang had taken £10 from Eley's pockets and Hurburgh's Austin Healey. Further up the road in Blackman's Lane was an abandoned green Triumph Spitfire stolen from Sydenham. It was not to the liking of the thieves. They had realised that it was too small for their purposes.

Alan Eley struggled across the fields to a house in Warlingham and raised the alarm but it was three o'clock by the time he succeeded in doing so and by then the gang were on their way to make yet another call.

The gang's next stop was at Limpsfield. They found an empty

cottage. New owners were due to move in shortly. Their packing cases were waiting for them in the house. It is likely that at this point the gang members called a halt to consider what next to do. In view of the fact that they had killed a man, perhaps they were uncertain whether they ought to continue with the night's plan – though 'plan' is perhaps too refined a word for their random descents on houses and people – or whether they ought to return home. As the night had so far netted them little – £10 and a car which they knew they would have to abandon – they decided to find another house to rob. They set off from Limpsfield with a radio and a telephone, all they had to show for their murderous activities.

Arriving at Oxted, five miles away, at about four o'clock, they chanced upon a substantial house in Woodhurst Lane, set in two acres of land. It must have seemed ideal for their needs. It obviously belonged to someone wealthy and must therefore yield something worthwhile. As it was away from other houses, there would be no fear of the neighbours being roused.

The gang found an unsecured window and made their entry to the house through it. The first that Richard Napier knew about their arrival was when he awakened to find a man wearing a balaclava shining a torch in his face. In his other hand the man held a handgun. Napier and his wife Margaret were ordered into the bedroom where his 40 year old son, Tim, was sleeping. Both men were then ordered to lie on the bed side by side, but an argument broke out, the Napier men resisting the man with the gun. Before the burglar had any opportunity to tie them up, both Napiers made a grab for the gun. They were later to admit that they believed it to be an imitation.

Grappling with the armed man they managed to force him out onto the landing but here they were alarmed to find two other intruders, their faces also masked. These two joined in the struggle and one of the burglars, drawing a knife, stabbed Tim Napier in the chest, back and arms. He had six stab wounds. Although losing a vast amount of blood he managed to find his way downstairs to call 999 but his voice was too faint for the operator who could only hear his laboured breathing. The number could not be immediately traced. Tim now collapsed from loss of blood from two severed arteries in his arm. But the gang were little concerned for him. Nor were they concerned for Margaret Napier whose rings they forced from her fingers with threats that they would have them even if her fingers had to be cut off. All the while Richard Napier was being threatened that if he did not do as they wished he would be shot.

Eventually Richard and Margaret were tied up while the gang made a hurried search of the house. They finally left with very little, so great was their anxiety to get away before there was any response to the emergency call. When the emergency service ambulance finally arrived they found Tim Napier in a critical condition, his slashed arm pouring blood. Only expert medical care at that stage and later in the East Surrey Hospital at Redhill avoided a second murder charge.

But the gang were undeterred. They took off in the Napiers' Toyota Corolla, this time leaving behind the Austin Healey. Up the motorway they went, still not sickened by what they had so far achieved that night, and apparently confident of their capacity to escape capture. They travelled 19 miles before their next stop at Fetcham near Leatherhead. At about 5.30 am they arrived at Hillyfield Lane where at gunpoint Rosemary Spicer and her boy friend, Peter Almond, were roused. They were dragged out of bed and bound. The house, a semi-detached property in great contrast to the Napiers' five-bedroomed home, was ransacked and jewellery, credit cards, cheque books and other items were stolen. The men made their escape in two cars from the house, a Vauxhall Cavalier hatchback and a Renault 5. Roadblocks, set up after the couple managed to call the police, failed to intercept the criminals.

On the Sunday, the two stolen cars were found blazing on a council rubbish heap at Foots Cray Meadow in Sidcup. Police were called but the two men who had been reported as starting the fire were not to be found.

As a consequence of this Thursday night-Friday morning rampage there was intense police activity. But in fact since the rape at Coulsdon on 5th December, a joint Metropolitan Police and Surrey Constabulary operation, led by Chief Superintendent Vincent McFadden, Head of the Surrey CID, had been working to identify the gang. It is worthy of mention that McFadden had benefited from Professor David Canter's contribution of the Psychological Offender Profile to the railway murders only three years earlier (see the chapter on The Railway Man) and that he brought to this investigation into murder, rape and violent robbery, an analytical approach which contributed to the capture of the gang. Thus, many seemingly minor details which might add to the general picture were considered. There was a firm conviction that the gang committed its raids high on drugs and adrenalin, thrilled to strike time and again and to be almost capture-proof. The detectives were convinced too that the mayhem along the M25 which had lasted a mere half dozen weeks or so, was not the only criminal activity that these men had been involved in. If they were not skilled burglars, they were at least practised in their trade. They were no mere beginners. Something like more than 90 offences were possibly attributable to them.

On the evening of Friday, 16th December, McFadden arranged a meeting at Reigate of senior detectives from Surrey and Scotland Yard. They were able to share further information about the gang and its behaviour in the Metropolitan Police area – at Coulsdon and Shirley, for instance – and within the Surrey Police boundaries at Ashtead and Fetcham, Fickleshole and Oxted. At this meeting new information was forthcoming.

Earlier in the day the police had issued the following descriptions of the wanted men:

FIRST MAN: White, long fair hair, uses a knife and machete.
SECOND MAN: White, mid-twenties, average height. Involved in a rape.
THIRD MAN: Black, stocky, mid-twenties. Carries a handgun to threaten victims.

Members of the public were warned not to approach the gang if they had any suspicions about their identity. A reward of £25,000 was offered for information to which Richard Napier added a further £5,000. He was rightly angered at what the gang had done to his wife and his son who was still not out of danger. 'They were ignorant and the scum of the earth,' he said, 'the lowest of the low. They should not exist.' To this Chief Superintendent McFadden added: 'It was gratuitous violence. I do not see how anyone could justify what these men did.'

Police were inundated with calls. On the Saturday night the incident room received more than 40 calls in three hours. Many suggested the identities of the gang members. Several calls came in from hardened criminals, sickened by the extraordinary level of violence. McFadden was delighted with the response. 'It is high quality information which has enhanced our enquiry,' he said. This information enabled the detectives to profile their quarry in behavioural and geographical terms with some confidence. Only 48 hours after the murder of Peter Hurburgh, McFadden felt able to order the arrest of suspects.

In the early hours of Sunday, 20th December, eleven men and a woman were taken for questioning from two addresses in Sydenham. More than 40 police officers including members of Scotland Yard's PT17 specialist firearms unit took part. Four men were arrested in connection with murder and eight others were held on 'associated matters'. There was a considerable amount of stolen property recovered, some of it related to several of the gang raids.

In the next week Michael George Davis, 22, and Raphael George Rowe, 20, both of them unemployed and both living at a social security hostel in Lawrie Park Road, Sydenham were remanded in custody on charges of murder, attempted murder and robbery. A third man, Randolph Johnson, escaped capture. At this time several others were being questioned about a series of violent crimes including rape. Jason Cooper, an 18 year old also living at Lawrie Park Road, was remanded in custody at Reigate charged with robbery at Ashtead, burglary at Croydon and the illegal possession of a firearm.

On Saturday, 7th January, Randolph Johnson aged 24 was charged at Dartford with the attempted murder of PC Hook whom he had taken hostage at gunpoint at Maidstone the previous day. He had shot at the policeman from a range of only four feet. He too was taken to Reigate for questioning relating to his part in the activities of the 'kill for kicks' gang.

The six-week trial of Davis, Rowe and Johnson, all of them black, all with serious criminal records, began on 16th January 1990. Mr Justice Auld made an order under the Contempt of Court Act that the accused were not to be named or identified in the media on the grounds that there might be other charges against them in another court. In late February they were found guilty of the murder of Peter Hurburgh, three counts of robbery and causing grievous bodily harm to the Napiers. On the direction of the judge they were acquitted of the attempted murder of Tim Napier.

Because of other charges – Johnson faced a charge of the attempted murder of PC Hook and of the rape of a Coulsdon housewife; Cooper charges of burglary and robbery – the judge still forbade any naming of the culprits.

On 30th March 1990, Randolph Johnson, Michael Davis and Raphael Rowe were jailed for life for the murder of Peter Hurburgh. In all they received a total of 275 years for their assaults on houses just off the motorway in South London, Surrey and Kent. Johnson was given 15 years for robbery, rape, possession of a firearm and causing grievous bodily harm. Rowe and Davis were also given concurrent sentences for robbery, causing grievous bodily harm and firearms offences. Lord Justice Auld described them as 'evil and dangerous men.'

The only white man charged, Jason Cooper, who took part in some of the raids, was given seven years for burglary and robbery.

An appeal by the three men in 1993 was unsuccessful after judges ruled that undisclosed police notes which cast doubt on the identity of the attackers were not a 'material irregularity'. But in 1999 the Criminal Cases Review Commission announced that the case was to be referred back once more to the Court of Appeal after it had received the results of an investigation it had ordered from Greater Manchester Police.

The case against the three black men was based, their supporters said, almost entirely on the evidence of three suspects who turned prosecution witnesses. No scientific or identification evidence linked them to these offences and fingerprints found at the murder scene did not match those of any of the convicted men. One of the witnesses of the attacks said two of the men involved were white and indeed, the notice issued by police to Surrey householders specifically mentioned that they sought two white and one black man.

In February 2000 the European Court of Human Rights expressed the view that the men had not been given a fair trial. The Crown had not been honest with the defence about one of their prime witnesses. This judgement was a break-through.

In July 2000, Lord Justice Mantell handed down the judgement of the Appeal Court which released the three men, all of them now in their thirties. Although the cases against them were 'formidable', he said, and in particular that against Rowe 'overwhelming', in the opinion of the court the convictions were not safe. 'They must be quashed and the appeal allowed.' But there is no doubt that the Appeal Court regarded their release a consequence of technicalities.

The Court found that detectives had conspired with a key witness, Norman Duncan, at the Old Bailey trial. Duncan, whose fingerprints had been found on one of the stolen cars, had appeared for the prosecution in return for £10,000 and immunity from any charges.

But the fact that Duncan was paid for his information had not been revealed at the time of the trial. 'It must,' said Lord Justice Mantell, 'dent the credibility of Duncan and the police directly involved.'

There was an additional irregularity which, had it been known, might have caused the Old Bailey trial to be aborted. The jury foreman had made unofficial visits to the robbery and murder sites. Whilst such behaviour may be regarded as an over-zealous error, the defence might have been inclined to make much of the matter. The Appeal judges had felt obliged to mention this too in their judgement.

Perhaps the last has not been heard of the infamous M25 gang or the investigation which led to the imprisonment of Johnson, Rowe and Davis. There were in the first hours of their release demands for further investigation of the way in which the enquiry had been carried out and suggestions that the men might claim compensation for wrongful imprisonment. They had been particularly stung by Lord Mantell's comment: 'This is not a finding of innocence – far from it.' After all, Davis and Rowe had tirelessly proclaimed their innocence for years. But the stain on their character is indelible.

So where does the truth lie? Are there men still free, men who have never been charged with the murder of Peter Hurburgh? Are they white men? Was their freedom assured by a deal with police? Did the wrong men go to prison for a murder they did not commit? To what extent were the men who were imprisoned implicated in those weeks of terror along the M25?

We may all have our own answers to these questions and our own opinions about what occurred in those late months of 1988. And it may be that we shall eventually discover the truth of the matter.

12

MONEY
TO BURN

The Murder of John Shippey at Croydon,
December 1991

John Shippey's life might have be-
longed within the covers of a novel in which he, generous almost
beyond belief, spread swathes of happiness among his friends. And if
he was able to be generous only because he was outrageously
dishonest, perhaps that was part of the man's undoubted charm. And in
the novel's conclusion he would get away with his frauds because he
was such an engaging character. No fiction writer would give a larger
than life character like John Shippey his come-uppance.

But John Shippey's murder, when he was terrified and helpless,
could have come out of another type of fiction.

For almost 18 months while Detective Chief Inspector John Beavis of
Surrey CID sought Shippey's murderer he learnt the histories – no, not
the *history* for this was a man whose life was more than one tale – of a
man whom he came to describe as 'enthralling.' This is not to say that
the detective approved of Shippey but that during the course of their
investigation, he and his team peeled away layer after layer of
deception with which the murdered man had covered up his
contradictory activities.

Beavis's interest in John Shippey began at Warwick Wold, near
Merstham. Late in the evening of 18th December 1991 the fire brigade
was called to a blazing car. Fire had almost totally destroyed the Sierra
Sapphire but when it was extinguished the firemen opened the boot
and discovered a body. A post-mortem revealed a slash wound on the
face and four stab wounds to the chest. Only dental records, however,
could determine the identity of the dead man. It was 47 year old John

Shippey, whose corpse had been burnt in his company car. Gas cylinders had been placed round the body before the car was set alight. Shippey had been reported missing three days earlier after he had not turned up for work.

Within days 28 year old Karl Watson was arrested but later released. There was no evidence against him. And so began a long investigation into the murder and the unfolding of a remarkable tale. Curiously in murder cases it does so often seem that the murderer is more interesting than the victim. Not so with John Shippey.

The murdered man was finance director with Dove's, Jaguar and Ford dealers in Croydon. Hard working, Shippey's capacity for work was matched by his capacity for pleasure. He was extremely well paid but even so, there were those who wondered how he could live such an extravagant life. Yet Shippey always disarmed his doubters. John Beavis spoke of the skill and charisma which helped him to avoid answering questions that could have led to his downfall.

How did he get away with it? What did he get away with? This was a man earning £40,000 a year. A good salary but could he really afford to spend such huge amounts giving parties for friends in top restaurants? And the designer suits? And always the two brief cases with sometimes up to £50,000 cash inside? Where did it all come from? And what about his substantial share in three houses in England and two apartments in Spain. Then there were the cars, the BMW, the Porsche and the Nissan. And in Spain the eight-berth motor cruiser, *John Boy*. And £180,000 in private accounts in Switzerland, Jersey, Spain and Gibraltar. According to Nigel Sweeney, prosecuting at the trial of the murderer, 'John Shippey was a trusted, popular and well-liked man.' And that is how he got away with it. Because no one could bring themselves to believe that he was such a massive crook. A sustained career of defrauding his employers over nine years and a good nose for wise investments enabled Shippey to amass a huge fortune. Four companies which he set up permitted him to siphon off, down unsuspected conduits, something in the order of £800,000. Think of the complex and meticulous records he had to maintain. Though the truth did not come out till after the murder.

Shippey's powerful and undoubtedly attractive personality allowed him to sustain close and loving relationships with three mistresses. He was an inveterate womaniser but his three principal women friends knew about each other and each accepted that it was her lot to be shared with the others. Shippey moved from one woman to another, spending a few nights here, a few nights there, depending on the state of the relationship. There is a sense in which he was not unfaithful for there was no deception in the the way he treated them. Whilst he had virtually separated from his wife, she lived in a select residential area and he made her generous financial allowances.

Another of his lady friends, with whom he had a seven year affair, said that he paid the £10,000 deposit on her house and for all of her furniture and that he regularly settled her credit card bills. He even took her on fortnightly shopping sprees. She was to say that it was because he was larger than life that many people loved Shippey. 'He got his kicks from taking risks,' she said. She told of how on one occasion when he had taken his wife to Spain, she had stayed in another apartment only a couple of hundred yards away. She said: 'He loved to take out his speedboat and wave at his wife on the beach with me crouching down beside him so I wouldn't be noticed.' Perhaps that suggests just a little less attractive side of the man everybody loved. Nor was she the only woman to be enthusiastic about the fun loving, free-spending Shippey.

But it was his mistress of 16 years, Jo Watson, to whom Shippey was most closely linked. He regularly spent a couple of nights with her each week. She had met him in the 1970s when she was a secretary at Dove's and their affair had not been damaged by his marriage to another member of staff. And as Shippey had prospered, so had she. He had paid a significant amount towards her £250,000 house at Ightham in Kent.

John Beavis was to sum up very perceptively the man whose life he had so closely studied in the course of the investigation. 'He lived his life in compartments and he didn't allow the people in each compartment to cross into others,' Beavis said, referring particularly to Shippey's financial universe. 'As far as we can tell he lived like this for most of his adult life. To manage to live like that he had to be intellectually very bright. He had to know which particular part of his life he was living each day but he kept it up. In material terms he was a success. He had everything anyone could wish for, several houses, several motor vehicles, several girl friends.' And so matters stood until 1991. John Shippey might have thought that they could go on this way for the rest of his life.

But Dove's new auditors were less than happy with the books. Suddenly Shippey was aware that he was under suspicion, that even his employers were uneasy about him. For the first time in years the world he had created for himself began to totter. His only hope was to try to realise enough cash to restore the funds he had so ruthlessly plundered. But he would need to act fast to put matters right. More than one witness was to describe his desperate anxiety in the weeks before the murder. Several others also noted the change as he strove to put his affairs in order. Shippey had begun to consider selling the three properties in England and the two in Spain. It was this solution which was to lead to his murder.

Jo Watson at Ightham was concerned that she would lose the house she had invested so much in. It was not all Shippey's money that had paid for it. And if Shippey and Jo Watson were desperate for the future so too was Jo Watson's son, Karl, now 29 and involved in car repairs and building.

Karl Watson, who lived in Croydon, had known Shippey for 16 years, ever since the relationship between the wealthy finance director and his mother had begun. And Watson hated the man. They had frequent spats over quite trivial matters when they met. Perhaps Watson was now concerned that his mother was to lose all she had striven for. More likely his own greed encouraged his murder plan. He envied Shippey's wealth and aimed to have some of it before it all disappeared.

What precisely occurred at Ightham late in the evening of 15th December 1991, is not known save that Karl Watson overpowered Shippey and bound and gagged him. He drove his prisoner to a lock-up garage in Croydon and then contacted a friend, 24 year old Bruce Cousins, who was to describe himself in court as Watson's 'gofer'. Cousins was told to go to the lock-up 'and look after the place or look after the bloke, I'm not sure which.' When he arrived there late at night, Cousins found a blue Sierra and inside, a man tied up in the back seat. He was gagged with broad brown tape and his eyes were covered with cotton wool also held on with tape. The prisoner's hands were tied behind his back with plastic cable ties and his feet were bound with tape. His shoes had been taken off.

Cousins spoke in court about the bitter cold in the lock-up. He had felt some sympathy for the man but no doubt for himself, too. He had gone home for a fan heater and when he returned had plugged it in near the car, leaving the door open so that Shippey could gain some benefit from the heat. In the course of an uncomfortable night Cousins must have recalled an earlier conversation when Watson had proposed kidnapping someone who owed him money. It would teach him a lesson, Watson said, but Cousins had refused to take part though he did offer to drive Watson to his destination. Cousins said he had not taken the proposal seriously 'because Karl was always boasting he'd done things'. Nevertheless, he might at the same time have remembered that Watson had a frightening reputation. What was he going to do with Shippey? Nothing to worry about, Watson reassured him, when he came to the lock-up at nine the next morning.

But John Shippey, his gag off but still bound, must have known of the unreliable temper of Karl Watson. And must have known how much the man hated him. He lay now in the front seat of the car while Watson taunted him, threatening and demanding money. It can only be imagined that Shippey tried to explain that it was all too late, that there was no longer the kind of money available that Watson was demanding. And it can be imagined also that Shippey begged for his life. Perhaps Watson, enraged, frustrated, realising that his plan could not work, wondered now what would be the best way out of the predicament he was in. It was unlikely that Shippey would have pressed charges against him if he was freed. After all, he had enough to concern himself with and in any case, to charge Watson would only encourage him to tell what he knew of Shippey's financial affairs. So Watson had a choice. Shippey need not have died.

But he did.

Watson went suddenly berserk, dragging Shippey from the front to the rear seat of the car. He told Cousins to pick up a 6″ kitchen knife which was on the roof of the car, ordering him to stab Shippey. When the young man refused, Watson took the knife, shouting, 'You should have paid', and stabbed Shippey several times in the chest.

Cousins, appalled, asked what was going to happen to the bleeding man. 'It's okay,' Watson answered. ' He's going to die.'

And when John Shippey did die they picked him up and slung him in the boot of his own car and motored it up to a lock-up garage in New Addington. Three days later, the car was set on fire at Warwick Wold.

Karl Watson, a man with a criminal record, was arrested within days and as promptly released as there was no evidence. Nevertheless, the police believed that they knew who had murdered John Shippey.

In September 1992 Bruce Cousins was arrested on another offence and unexpectedly elected to tell the police all they wished to know about the abduction, murder and final disposal of John Shippey. Perhaps the awful events of that morning in the Croydon lock-up had preyed on his mind. Within a week Karl Watson was arrested.

In December 1993, Karl Watson appeared at the Old Bailey charged

Karl Watson who was found guilty of the murder of John
Shippey (courtesy of News International Syndication).

with false imprisonment and the murder of John Shippey. The father of
four denied the charges. But there was strong evidence against him.
There was one of Shippey's brief cases in yet another of his rented
lock-ups. There were fragments of the dead man's Dannimac coat in
the ashes of his garden bonfire. There was the witness to whom he had
boasted: 'I took care of him. I burned the fat bastard.' The case against
Watson was irresistible.

Karl Watson was found guilty and sentenced to a minimum of 20
years. Judge Nina Lowry spoke of his deliberate, calculated cruelty.
'Anyone capable of such cruelty against a fellow human being may
repeat it,' she said. Yes, he might.

Like a work of fiction? Yes, but sadly all too real.

13

LUST
FOR DEATH

The murder of Robert Wignall at Addlestone,
September 1992

Everybody spoke highly of Bob
Wignall. As his wife said at the time, 'He was a very kind man, very
caring.' And Detective Superintendent Pat Crossan, in charge of the
case, recalled that they had not been long married. 'They were widow
and widower,' he said, 'but they obviously found love, affection and
happiness together and that has now been shattered.' Shattered indeed
on 5th September 1992, in the same woods at Addlestone where they
had met, walking their dogs in the woodlands that Bob had always
loved. Together, Sandra Wignall said, they had found solace in their
loneliness.

That evening at about 9.30, just before dusk, they had gone out of the
garden gate of their house in Rowhurst Avenue straight into Sayes
Wood. They had taken scraps for three fox cubs that they knew would
be there. Sandra told the detective how they had just put down the
scraps when three young men came from behind the bushes. She was
immediately uneasy, she said, meeting them there at that time of night.
One of the men asked, 'Have you seen a boxer dog puppy?' but before
either she or Bob could reply, the men began verbally abusing her
husband, yelling, swearing at him. Suddenly, without warning, they
attacked him, shoving and pushing until he was knocked off balance.
This unwarranted attack had terrified Sandra and she fled, fearing that
she too was to be a victim. Her husband's voice, urging her to escape,
followed her. 'That was the calibre of the man,' Crossan said, 'that he
would think of his wife's safety at that time.' Bob Wignall had sacrificed
his life for his wife, the policeman told the public.

Terrified, Sandra hid in the bushes and then only when the men had gone did she return to find her husband's body lying in the copse where she had left him, only yards from his home. He had been stabbed and bludgeoned to death in what was described as a 'particularly vicious and brutal' attack. His clothing was saturated with blood from two knife wounds to the heart and another in the neck. His face had been battered with a blunt instrument.

Some time later three young men, Richard Vinnicombe aged 19, his brother Stephen and their friend Nathan Burkitt found her near her husband's body. At the trial months later Richard told how some minutes earlier they had passed two men walking through Sayes Wood. Speaking of their meeting with Sandra Wignall, Richard said, 'We came across her in a clearing. She was moving around backwards and forwards. She was not saying anything. First of all she said "Stay away", then something like "Stay away, stay back."' She had then told them of the attack on her husband.

The police were anxious to involve the public in their investigation. Only days after the murder, members of the dead man's family gave an interview at a conference called by Detective Superintendent Crossan. Debbie Philpot spoke admiringly of her father. 'I never knew him raise his hand or argue with anyone,' she said. 'He was just a nice man.' Sandra was too upset to go to the conference. 'She still rehearses the incident over and over in her mind,' the public was told. This kind of public exposure was very effective. From the earliest days of Detective Superintendent Crossan's investigation members of the public telephoned and wrote in with information which gave him extraordinarily useful pointers. The police received over 300 responses by letter or telephone. Who could fail to be moved at the story of a couple married only the previous year on Christmas Eve? Now, after only nine months, brutal murderers had ruined the life that the couple were making together.

There was also extensive newspaper coverage of the apparently motiveless murder of the 55 year old painter and decorator. Great emphasis was placed on the essentially decent man, a gentle animal and nature lover, a man described as 'charming, gracious, very well mannered, a man of honour.' No doubt it was this in part which encouraged such a good response from the public.

Early in their search of the scene of the attack the police found a cheap gold bracelet, the kind worn by a man. Attached to it were threads from Bob Wignall's jumper. The owner of that piece of jewellery had the answer to what exactly had happened in Sayes Wood on that early September evening.

While supporting the distraught 47 year old widow and talking her carefully through what had occurred, Pat Crossan reflected on what she was telling him, seeking for small hints, odd clues to a crime which on the face of things was without reason. Despite her grief Sandra had been able to give him a meticulous description of the attackers. They were in their twenties. One had worn a baseball cap, another had a particular motif on his jeans. She was able to describe the colours of the men's shirts. And yet, as the detective and his team thought about it, was not the description too complete? Would a woman in a twilit copse, placed so suddenly in such danger, really have been able to take in such detail? Would she not have been too afraid to absorb such matters? She said that she had screamed when first the men began attacking her husband but why had no one else heard her? It was a summer's evening. There were other people about. Surely they must have heard her.

The experience of policemen inclines them to be sceptical of much of what they hear. Perhaps what Sandra said was absolutely true but Crossan's instincts made him cautious so that while he initiated the search for the three men she had described, he began delving into her background. Even so, whilst he made these surreptitious enquiries, he encouraged her to make an appeal on TV's *Crime Monthly*. This too was to produce further useful background material on Sandra Wignall.

The widow's plausible act of bitter grief was quickly losing its effect on Crossan the more information came in to him. Yet he made no move to indicate to her that he doubted the truth of her story. He continued patiently looking for the two men who had been seen in the wood, one of whom he was sure had lost the identity chain. These were dangerous men and he did not wish to lose them. In the meantime when the distraught widow tried very early to cash her late husband's insurance policy Crossan felt that this hinted at a motive.

In the two or three weeks following the murder more and more useful information crossed the Superintendent's desk. One thing he knew about Sandra Wignall was that she was a gossip. And more and more of those who knew her began to put two and two together and horrified, passed their thoughts to the police. For example, Crossan learnt that only two days before the murder Sandra and Bob had had a row. He had been checking the mileometer on her car. It just did not tally with her claims that she was driving only locally during the day.

She swore that she limited her driving to the shops in Woking or Weybridge. But if that was the case, Bob had asked, why such a high mileage and why, he wanted to know, was she away from home two or three times a week for up to five or six hours each time. Where was she going? Was she seeing Terry Bewley, her old lover? When they checked, the police found that Bewley had a long criminal record. He was a highly dangerous man. Relatively early in the investigation, having heard about this argument, the police decided to keep a close watch on Sandra and Terry Bewley.

Sandra had apparently resumed her liaison with Bewley even before Bob Wignall's funeral. But then she had scarcely given it up since she was married. Had they planned the murder in Sayes Wood? If so, there must have been a second man. Crossan was sure of that. One had stabbed, the other had used a weapon to beat the man to death.

A watch was now kept on Terry Bewley's Ruislip home. By mid-October the police discovered that he was in touch with Harold Moult, a 42 year old petty criminal who lived in Hockley, West Midlands. When detectives called on him, Moult was rattled, shifty. He could not remember where he was on 5th September. No, he said, he had not lost a bracelet, but reminded that his fingerprints would be on it, he confessed without hesitation.

He and Bewley had hidden in the wood. Sandra and Bob had come through the garden gate and into the clearing. Moult said that Sandra had distracted Bob and that was when they came out of hiding. At the last moment Bob looked round and saw his killers, Moult told the police: 'Terry said something to him and the next thing I knew they were on the floor fighting. I stepped in. I hit him. I think I hit him with a piece of wood over the head. I saw a knife and I am not sure if I picked the knife up and the bloke came at me. I might have stabbed him. I am not sure.'

That was Moult's version. 'I think ... I am not sure ... I might have ... I am not sure ...' But he could remember Bob Wignall's last words: 'Please do not stab me.'

After the murder Bewley set fire to the car that he had borrowed to destroy any signs of blood. Moult threw the knife away in a canal and he was able to take the officers to the spot. He had taken their bloodstained clothing home and had burned it in his back garden.

On 30th October, almost two months after her husband's dreadful death, Sandra Wignall was charged with conspiracy to kill. Terry Bewley and Harold Moult were charged with murder.

The court case revealed a sordid tale. Sandra had married Bob Wignall more or less on the rebound from the love of her life. Since 1989 she had adored Bewley, had been obsessed with him. Whilst she was sexually promiscuous to an extreme degree and had had countless affairs of which she frequently boasted, her choice of Terry Bewley for a lover is at first sight surprising. He was certainly an unlikely looking ladies' man. At 43, the balding, thick-set, bespectacled Bewley who worked as a chauffeur was generally short of cash. Divorced, he had a child by another woman. In the summer of 1992 he was deeply in debt, owing £30,000. How could he repay the money unless he resorted to desperate measures? And Sandra was so obsessed by Bewley that she would forgive him anything. He could treat her disdainfully but she did not care. This added spice to their love-making, for sex, the dominant element in her life, was with Bewley like no other experience she had ever known. This was a woman with an insatiable sexual appetite, a woman who had taken part in bizarre sexual experiments. It is said that on the day of her second husband's funeral in 1985 – he had died of cancer – she was found in bed with a man. She was constantly on the look-out for casual pick-ups. But no one matched the prowess and the attraction of Terry Bewley.

So Bewley could borrow money from Sandra and she never complained. Before her marriage to Bob Wignall she had lent him £4,000, her entire savings, and it had never been repaid. At one point she had to sell her car to make ends meet as a result of the sacrifices she had to make for Terry Bewley. There was a time when she had even considered selling her house in Addlestone and moving into a mobile home in order to settle his debts. Yet she did not even have his address or telephone number in Ruislip. No, that was private, he told her. That was his business. And reluctantly she accepted the situation. The man had a demonic sexual spell over Sandra.

Sandra had first met Bewley when he was driving expensive cars for Prince Bassye of Nigeria. It is enough to say that Bewley borrowed £10,000 from his employer and this was never repaid. Later he was chauffeur to Sheikh Mohammed Hamdan Maktoum, a wealthy race-horse owner. During breaks from driving his employers and their friends around in Rolls-Royces, Bewley would fit in meetings with Sandra. He would phone her at Addlestone. 'Get in your car,' he would tell her. 'Wear a coat but be naked underneath.' She had photographs taken by Bewley of the two of them having sex in one of the cars. She passed these around her friends. On one occasion, on her way to meet

Bob Wignall and his wife Sandra at their wedding reception (courtesy of Cassidy & Leigh).

him, her car had broken down. Embarrassed and distressed, and flimsily dressed, she had had to call a garage much to the amusement of passers-by. Nevertheless, undeterred, when Bewley made the same request some days later she did as she was asked. And none of these matters was kept from anyone who cared to listen.

At the trial, Sandra's neighbour, Christine Willis, revealed that Sandra had told her that Bewley enjoyed watching her have sex with strangers. After a row, when she had not seen him for several weeks, Bewley turned up unannounced at her house one day. He had a gift for her, he said. He had blindfolded and bound her to the bed. Then he had introduced two strangers who joined her in the bed. She claimed that she did not enjoy the experience but that she would do anything to keep her lover.

Only nine days after her marriage to Bob Wignall, Sandra resumed her liaison with Bewley. Marriage to Bob was a mistake, she claimed. Oh, he was a decent enough man but not her type. He was asthmatic and not as sexually active as she wanted; not as sexually active as she needed. Within a couple of weeks or so, she was dropping Bob off at work and then going to Bewley whenever he sent for her. She could not do without him. She was, she said, depressed if she could not meet him and she was increasingly tired of her husband's devotion.

And she worried more and more about her lover's financial difficulties. And so the murder plan was hatched. There was an insurance of £20,000 on Bob's life. That would be the solution to Bewley's problem and to her own, for as she told her friends and whoever seemed to want to listen to her at the hairdresser's where she was a regular customer, she regretted her marriage increasingly. And perhaps after, she and Bewley could settle down to a normal life. But murder? That was a step she had not taken before. No doubt Bewley encouraged her. After all he was a convicted killer. In 1972 he had received a life sentence for strangling a woman debt-collector in Tottenham. He had served eleven years in prison.

Now Bewley was going to resolve another of his money problems. He and Moult and Sandra had discussed the plan. Bob and she would come out of the house at twilight. Once in the wood, she would distract him ... It was all so simple. All Sandra had to do was to lead her unsuspecting husband to his death.

But Sandra Wignall had talked too much. Too many people knew that she had a lover, that she was sick of her husband.

In 1993, all three received life sentences for their truly dreadful crime.

116

Nor did any of them appear to show any remorse. In 1994, Harold Moult died from a deliberate drug overdose at Gartree Prison in Leicestershire. In the same year Sandra Wignall was refused leave to appeal against her conviction.

14

THE
PIZZA MAN

The Murder of Karen Reed at Woking,
April 1994

'**H**ave you ordered a pizza?' he asked.
He stood in the doorway, a small blue and white box in his hand.

Karen hadn't. She turned to Ann to confirm that she hadn't either.

Was this the right address, he asked. Perhaps he had the wrong number, he said.

Well, he had the right house, Karen told him, but neither of them had...

That was when she heard the shots, Ann Smith was to tell the police later, six of them in quick succession. 'I realised it was a gun,' she said. 'I ran upstairs because I knew there was a panic alarm in the house because of the situation with Karen's sister.' But upstairs, she was unable to find the button and raced back down to dial 999. Then she went to Karen who lay on her back by the front door. There were six bullet wounds in her chest, side and back. She had been shot at point blank range. By the time the ambulance came, Karen was dead. And the pizza man had sped off into the night.

So it was that on 30th April 1994 Russian gangsters made their mark in Woking, in suburban Willow Way, on the Barnsbury Park estate. Karen Reed, a 33 year old geophysicist who worked at Addlestone, was murdered by a hitman whose paymaster was 2,000 miles away. And she was the wrong target for it was her sister Alison who was the intended victim. But Alison was working at the BBC that evening and her sister failed to take the precautions that the police had advised. They knew that Alison was in possible danger. They had warned the sisters not to open the door to strangers and had even gone so far as to

118

Artist's impression of the killer.

install security equipment in the house. But out of thoughtlessness perhaps, possibly because it is really difficult sometimes to believe that foreign killers could ever roam our streets, when the door bell rang at 9.15 that April evening, without any hesitation Karen went to the front door to meet the pizza man.

'It has all the hallmarks of a professional killing,' said Detective Superintendent John Stewardson who was in charge of the investigation. The killer, somewhere in his mid-thirties according to Ann Smith, was about six feet tall, dark haired, wearing metal rimmed spectacles. And whilst the general description might suggest someone from the Middle East, he spoke with a good English accent. Had he been recruited nearer to home? If the question of the killer's identity remained unanswered – and it remains so today – the tangled roots of the doorstep murder were clear. And there had been warnings enough that something dreadful was likely to happen. Alison Ponting had no doubt that she had been the intended victim. Karen had been murdered so horrifically because the assassin had mistaken her for her sister. They were much alike to look at, both had mousy hair, both wore spectacles.

Only two weeks earlier there had been the incident of the car. Police had chased a red Vauxhall Cavalier with false number plates through the Barnsbury Park estate. The driver had leapt from the moving car and escaped into neighbouring woodland. The car had been stolen in Uxbridge 18 months earlier and the bloom on the paintwork suggested that it had been kept with its rear under cover and its front out in the open. Not another joy rider then. In any case joy riders do not usually leave commando knives behind them. Nor do they leave holdalls on the passenger seat. At least, not holdalls with automatic pistols inside them. And certainly they do not leave automatic pistols with silencers. There were bullets too for the weapon. And these had been specially prepared. They had been hollowed out, filled with liquid mercury and stopped with wax. Such expertise indicates someone professional, someone aware that these kinds of bullets increase the explosive impact, that they inflict fatal injuries wherever they hit. This incident took place at about nine o'clock. Was it a rehearsal for what occurred a fortnight later?

It was the map inside the abandoned car which alerted the Surrey police to the quite unprecedented situation. For the map had on it a number of marks which though imprecise led them to the conclusion that some people on the estate were in danger. When they considered

DEADLY

The killer's gun and silencer both measured 15cms (or six inches)

The type of weapon used by the assassin.

the situation they felt able to pinpoint certain potential targets, five families whom they warned to take care and in whose homes they installed state-of-the-art security devices. Among those whom they assumed to be in some kind of danger were bank staff and people involved in security. And there was Alison Ponting, who at the time was living with her sister Karen.

Alison Ponting, who had taken a Russian degree at Manchester, had met her art dealer husband in Armenia. After their marriage in 1988 they had come to live in England. Alison had joined the BBC World Service Russian and Ukrainian desk and by 1991 had become a producer. Gagic Ter-Ogrannsyan, her husband, had continued his art dealing, smuggling some works out of Russia, and he was also involved in oil sales. A successful entrepreneur, he was a man of substantial wealth. And then onto the scene came Ruslan Outsiev, the self-styled premier of Chechenya, the tiny oil-rich state in the Caucasus.

Chechenya is a couple of hours' flying time from Moscow. It is a remote, mountain land, flush with oil revenues from which some Chechens benefit and from which more do not. Here, side by side, are extreme poverty and excessive wealth. Here are poor, proud, independent mountain people, sometimes ruthless and unforgiving, and here are equally ruthless and unforgiving politicians on the make. And with feet in both camps there are the Chechen gangsters in their fancy suits, with their flashy cars and their all too visible Kalashnikovs. It is a volatile and dangerous region. And as the Chechen gangsters have the reputation of being so much more ferocious than others in the world of the lawless, they hold the Russian underworld in their grip. They are allegedly the world's most ruthless killers. So a Russian general is shot in Moscow; a liberal MP is killed; another MP is kidnapped and murdered; a respected TV journalist is shot; a contract killer takes out a bank director. The central power in the Russian underworld comes from these Chechen criminals who are behind much of the decline in law and order in the former Soviet Union. They control by brutal means many of the legal and most of the major illegal enterprises in Russia. And they spread their wings and export themselves, these frightening Chechens, and we hear of their presence in other parts of Europe including Britain. They are into the movement of illegal arms, into counterfeiting, into drug smuggling, into prostitution. They are, of course, a force in the government of their own land.

In 1992 Ruslan Outsiev, a man in his late thirties, comes to London, accompanied by his 21 year old brother, Nazerbeck, a keep-fit fanatic. They have an agenda. They have come to Britain to make arrangements for the printing of bank notes, stamps and passports. They have come to talk about oil, too, and they are looking for a site for the Chechen Embassy for they are contemplating that their small republic will sever itself entirely from the Russian state. Outsiev is also looking for Stinger surface to air missiles, 2,000 of them. It is thought that he may arrange for these to be sold on to his fellow Muslims in Azerbaijan so that they can wage war on Christian Armenia. Or perhaps they are to be used by the Chechens themselves if Mother Russia proves intransigent. It is certainly a long shopping list and a costly one too. But Chechenya can afford it. Chechenya has oil.

Chechenya can even afford its prime minister and his young brother who are living it up in fine style. There is more to spend on in London than in Moscow. And as for Grozny, their puny capital, that has nothing to offer. So restaurant bills for £2,000 are paid without demur. Waiters are given £100 tips when Outsiev foots the bill. The four-bedroomed flat off Baker Street which cost £750,000 and which took three days for Harrods to fill with furnishings amounting to £90,000, never quietens. There are constant parties, dinners, meetings, as well as regular processions of prostitutes of the more expensive kind. But oil money runs freely.

Not surprisingly the flamboyant Ruslan Outsiev was interviewed on the BBC World Service. By Alison Ponting who had, equally unsurprisingly, retained her maiden name. After this her husband, seeking more contacts for his various enterprises, was introduced to Outsiev and did some interpreting and translation for him. It was undoubtedly lucrative work. But then matters changed.

In March 1993 delivery men were called to move a heavy wooden box containing what they were told was a valuable statue from the Outsievs' flat to a garage in Harrow. The men found the pungent stench emanating from the box not only unpleasant but downright suspicious. They called the police. Inside the box was Outsiev's trussed-up body. He had been shot in the head three times. Young Nazerbeck's body was in the Marylebone flat. He too had taken three head shots. Detectives, alerted to the situation, kept a watch on the flat and arrested two men returning from a DIY store where they had been buying saws with the clear intention of dismembering the second corpse.

One was Gagic Ter-Ogrannsyan, Alison Ponting's husband; the other Mcritch Martirossian. They had formerly been partners in the art trade in Russia and had recently been reunited when Martirossian arrived in Britain. Martirossian was on his own admission a member of the Armenian KGB. It has been denied that Ter-Ogrannsyan belonged to that organisation but both were involved in the murder of the Outsiev brothers. They were under KGB orders to kill them when it became apparent that Chechenyan money was going to buy Stinger missiles. An attempt by peaceful means to dissuade Outsiev had failed.

After he was arrested Martirossian gave some insight into the ruthless nature of his superiors. 'The murders were planned by the KGB,' he said. 'I had no choice but to obey the KGB. They would have harmed my family.' And they expected even more of him now that he had been caught and was awaiting trial. Snake venom which Martirossian's masters had expected him to take on arrest had been confiscated by the police. But the price of failure in the world in which the Armenian moved is high. He was visited by his spymaster, a KGB general, whilst on remand at Belmarsh top security prison. The next day Martirossian was found hanged in his cell.

Gagic Ter-Ogrannsyan was given two life sentences for his part in the murder of the Outsiev brothers though it is doubtful that he pulled the trigger. Perhaps what he had done was make it possible for his old friend to murder the Chechens. At no point was it suggested that he belonged to the Armenian KGB.

Either the world of international organised crime or of powerful secret policemen came to Woking and turned up at Willow Way on that April evening in 1994. Perhaps it was a combination of both for who knows where one world begins and the other ends. Certainly the purpose of the killing was to teach a lesson, to exact revenge, to remind others that in such a dark and tangled world, distance is no object. Detective Superintendent Stewardson in charge of the investigation thought that perhaps Gagic Ter-Ogrannsyan's business deals with Chechens might have had some bearing on what had occurred. No one has yet been identified satisfactorily as gunman or paymaster. And despite extensive enquiries the police have been unable to penetrate a dense thicket of silence. Some people undoubtedly know some of the truth of why an innocent young woman was gunned down in suburbia. But they aren't saying. They daren't say. Not even today.

BIBLIOGRAPHY

During my research I consulted various books. I list them below with my grateful thanks to the authors.

Browne, DG, *Bernard Spilsbury*, Harrap, 1951.

Canter, David, *Criminal Shadows*, Harper Collins, 1994.

Cyriax, Oliver, *The Penguin Encyclopaedia of Crime*, Penguin, 1996.

Dernley, Syd, *Memoirs of a public Executioner*, Hale, 1989.

Farrell, Michael, *Poisons and Poisoners*, Hale, 1992.

Gaute, JHH and Odell, Robin, *Murder 'WhatDunnit'*, Pan, 1984.

Gaute, JHH and Odell, Robin, *The Murderers' Who's Who*, Harrap, 1979.

Goodman, Jonathan (ed), *Daily Telegraph Murder File*, Mandarin, 1993.

Goodman, Jonathan (ed), *The Railway Murders*, Sphere, 1986.

Jesse, F Tenneson (ed), *The Trial of Ley and Smith*, 1947.

Lane, Brian, *The Murder Guide*, Robinson, 1991.

Roberts, Tom, *Friends and Villains*, Hodder and Stoughton, 1987.

Simpson, Keith, *Forty Years of Murder*, Harrap, 1978.

Trow, MJ, *The Wigwam Murder*, Constable, 1994.

Tullett, Tom, *Murder Squad*, Diamond, 1996.

Ward, Jenny, *Crimebusting*, Blandford, 1998.

Whittington-Egan, Richard, *The Riddle of Birdhurst Rise*, Harrap, 1975.

INDEX